Loving God, Loving Myself

JERRY and **DENISE BASEL**

Authors of *The Missing Commandment: Love Yourself*

Loving God, Loving Myself

FINDING THE HEART of THE FATHER
in OUR DAILY LIVES

To our spiritual daughters and sons. Thank you for "adopting" us. You will always have a special place in our hearts.

CONTENTS

ACKNOWLEDGEMENTS

To God our Father: Thank you, Father, for allowing us to see deeper into your heart. Thank you for those you have brought to The Father's Heart Ministry and for trusting us with each one.

To our clients: Thank you for trusting us with your hearts and your lives. Your healing journeys and your life stories are very precious to us.

To our board members, our intercessors, our friends, and our families: Thank you for your love, your prayers, and your ongoing encouragement. We thank God for each one of you.

To our editor, Bob Hartig: It was a blessing to have you working with us again on this project. Your heart for God and your editing ability are a special gift.

And to all who have been utilizing *The Missing Commandment: Love Yourself* materials—including those who have been facilitating classes and small groups: We are grateful and humbled by the stories of how the Father has met so many of you personally and brought forth more of his healing love. It brings joy to us and to the Father!

INTRODUCTION

Welcome to our book, *Loving God, Loving Myself: Finding the Father's Heart in Our Daily Lives*. We're excited that you've decided to join us as we share our hearts on this journey.

After reading and working through our initial book, *The Missing Commandment: Love Yourself—How Loving Yourself the Way God Does Can Bring Healing and Freedom to Your Life*, many have asked us if we had another resource to help them continue on the road to wholeness. What you have in front of you is our response.

The writings we share in this book are personal to us yet globally relevant to others. Some of you were previously introduced to us through our first book; for others, *Loving God, Loving Myself* may be your first exposure to our writings. No matter where you are in the healing journey—whether at the beginning, middle, or end—we believe the Father will meet you exactly where you are.

Loving God, Loving Myself is a compilation of fifty-five inspirational readings that correspond with the eleven chapter topics in *The Missing Commandment: Love Yourself*. However, you need not read these in that order. Each reading stands alone. So while it might also be helpful for you to have previously read our first book, it is not necessary. The one thing that we *do* recommend is that you take your time reading each of these writings. Allow the Father to sit with you and share his heart with you as you read.

Some of these writings come from the stories of those we have helped along the way (specifics have been changed to protect anonymity). Others come from stories we have read. Still others have come directly from our personal stories. The common element in these writings is *story*—something we see throughout the Bible, and something that is very important in all of our lives.

Some of the writings are inspirational. Others are informative and instructional to help you better understand yourself and your life story. Some ask questions that invite you to search your heart and seek God for his truth. Others are meant to encourage you that you are not alone on your journey.

The writings are of various lengths—some short, others longer. We hope you will find a nugget of insight in each one, and a time to laugh, to ponder, and to take in a deep breath of the Father's feelings and his heart for you.

When you come to the prayers we have at the end of each reading, allow them, when possible, to become *your* prayers. And in all of this, take time to stop, listen, feel, and write down what comes—maybe even to write a letter or two to God or to relevant others. To assist you, we have included a page at the end of every writing for your thoughts and reflections. We believe that approaching the book this way will give you the most benefit as you continue the journey of healing and transformation.

All the Father needs in this process is your willing heart to choose him and receive all he has in his heart for you. He is love, and you are *his* love. And when you know your identity deep down inside, the revelation of your destiny follows.

So again, welcome. Join us as we travel this road together to be and become all we are meant to be in him. It is our hope and our prayer that you will indeed love God, love yourself, and find more of the Father's heart in your daily life.

WEEK ONE

LOVE WHAT GOD LOVES

*There is nothing more important in either the Old
or New Testaments of the Bible, in terms of what God asks of
us, than to love him and to love others as we love ourselves.*
— The Missing Commandment: Love Yourself

In Mark 12:28–31, Jesus is asked which of the commandments is the most important. He replies, "Love the Lord your God with all your heart and with all your soul and with all your mind and with all your strength." He continues, "The second is this: 'Love your neighbor as yourself.' There is no commandment greater than these." There is nothing more important in either the Old or the New Testaments of the Bible, in terms of what God asks of us, than to love him and to love others as we love ourselves.

We seem to get most of this. We are to love God and we are to love others. But where we, Jerry and Denise, see so many falling short on understanding and living out this teaching is in the area of loving ourselves.

Ask yourself, "Do I love others to the same degree or in the same way or manner that I love myself?" There is supposed to be no difference. None. And we believe this understanding is missing in great part in the church and in the lives of those who seek to follow Christ. We further believe—based on our own lives and the lives of those we have counseled—that it is not possible to do a good job of keeping the first commandment, loving God, without fulfilling all of the second.

Loving what God loves is the key—and he absolutely loves you.

PRAYER FOR THE JOURNEY

As we begin Week One, pray with us for the Father's loving guidance in the journey ahead:

Father, open my heart and help me see what you want me to see concerning this issue of loving myself. As I begin this journey into my heart, I need to know more of your heart. Help me to see if this commandment has been missing in my life, and if so, help me to find and restore what has been lost or disregarded. You pursue lost things (Luke 15), and you pursue me so that I can live from a restored heart. I want to be able to fully love you, myself, and others. I trust you in this journey.

LOVING WHO GOD LOVES

Love what God loves. Hate what God hates.
And don't get them mixed up.
—Jerry Basel

As we read and study Scripture, there always seems to be a place that hits home. We have to stop and think, pondering its meaning for our personal lives. Matthew 22:37–39 is a profound and hugely significant example. Asked what the greatest commandment of Scripture is, Jesus replies that it is to love the Lord with everything in us, and that the second commandment, similar to the first, is to love our neighbor as we love ourselves.

As we love ourselves. Let's pause here a second. If the love I show my neighbor equals the *lack* of love I have for myself, what does that suggest? I'm thinking that a lot of my neighbors aren't getting much love from me. And Jesus says that everything hangs on these two commandments. Everything.

What does it take to overcome the obstacles to loving ourselves the way God does—a way that frees us to love others fully and freely with his own incredible love?

God reveals his life-giving heart toward us in endless ways, from times spent studying and meditating on his Word to unique moves of the Holy Spirit.

A friend's daughter shared with us her firsthand experience at a college in the Midwest. While she and her fellow students were listening to the teacher and taking notes, suddenly God's presence filled the room. Twelve hours later, they were still in the classroom. The Father was healing their hearts, freeing them from self-hatred, guilt, and shame. And what unfathomable freedom comes when God heals a broken heart!

Our own journey of the heart began in 1995, when we started our counseling ministry, The Father's Heart. It was founded on the first and greatest commandment. We were committed to helping others love God with their whole heart and remove any hindrances—pain, hurt, betrayal, fear, rejection, walls, generational sin, pride, unforgiveness. We said, "If people are emotionally healed in our ministry but are not any closer to God when they leave, then we have failed."

Then seventeen years later, Father God turned the page to the second commandment: to love others as we love ourselves. I (Denise) was in the middle of making our bed, minding my own business, when out of nowhere the words dropped into my head: *the missing commandment—love yourself.* "Wow, I could write a book about that!" I thought. And over the next several months, Jerry and I did just that.

Maybe today is a new day for you—a new season of learning to love who God made you to be. The *true* you without all the baggage—the old patterns of relating, the lies, the fortified walls, the mask. Now is a time for you to begin, with God, to sort through the developmental stages of your childhood. You have to go back to your childhood, because what occurred there is the development of *you.* Doing this takes a vulnerable heart, yielded to the Father, who is truth. He is waiting for your signal to begin the journey. Just say yes. He'll plan the rest.

PRAYER

Father, it is still profoundly good news that "Jesus loves me, this I know." It is profoundly good news that, as my loving Father, you desire to heal my self-hatred, self-condemnation, self-contempt, self-rejection, and negative self-talk. I want to come into agreement with who you say I am.

Now look in the mirror and repeat these affirmations to God aloud:

I am precious in your sight.
I am your delight.
I am your child.
I am a jewel in your crown.
I am your handiwork.

When you are able to love yourself the way God loves you, you can say at last, "I am truly free to become fully me."

THOUGHTS AND REFLECTIONS

*When we love ourselves, we will experience greater peace and joy in life.
Then we will be able to fulfill the destiny that God places within us.*

CAN YOU LOVE YOURSELF TOO MUCH?

Christianity does not come in order to develop the heroic virtues in the individual, but rather to remove self-centeredness and establish love.
—Soren Kierkegaard

Can you love yourself too much?

It's a surprising question, but it's one we've been asked. We never anticipated it would be a counseling issue. Yet we have read personal commentaries and heard people express their opposition to the teaching that we should love ourselves: "We already do that too much. This is the problem in our churches and in the world."

What do people mean when they think of loving oneself too much? Some might picture a person who is arrogant, controlling, and always certain she is right. She looks down on others because she thinks so highly of herself.

On the other hand, there is the individual who is needy for affection, attention, and emotional support—self-absorbed. He wants people to take care of him and wait on him. This person may be judged as loving himself too much because of his self-centeredness: "It's always about him."

Look closely at the characteristics of each kind of person—both the puffed-up and the needy—and you will find things missing from God's description of what love looks like:

Love endures with patience *and* serenity.

Love is kind *and* thoughtful, and is not jealous *or* envious.

Love does not brag and is not proud *or* arrogant.

It is not rude.

It is not self-seeking.

It is not provoked [nor overly sensitive and easily angered].

It does not take into account a wrong *endured*.

It does not rejoice at injustice, but rejoices with the truth [when right and truth prevail].

Love bears all things [regardless of what comes].

Love believes all things [looking for the best in each one].

Love hopes all things [remaining steadfast during difficult times].

Love endures all things [without weakening]

(1 Cor. 13:4–7, adapted from AMP).

If God says this is what love is, I wouldn't mind living in a world that loves "too much." With his definition of love, there could only be one person who could ever have the capacity and perfection that way—God himself. When he describes himself, he says, "I am love" (1 John 4:8, 16). And that is more than enough.

God has a plan for those who are self-centered, prideful, arrogant, self-absorbed. It is called healing—healing from a wound caused by a lack of love, affection, affirmation, belonging, safety, encouragement, and guidance when a child was growing up.

So can you love yourself too much? According to the Father, absolutely not.

PRAYER

Father, you've called me to love you, myself, and others. Please help me to see love the way you do. I need your definition of love and nothing else. Forgive me for the times when I have misused this word and misrepresented it to others. And help me also to extend grace to those who are operating from a wound and speaking against the very thing that is central to your heart—loving ourselves and each other. When confronted with this attitude, help me to pray for them rather than judge. Thank you, Father, for being love.

THOUGHTS AND REFLECTIONS

The ability to love ourselves is biblical. But more than just biblical, it is an essential truth for us to believe, experience, and live out.

GOD WITH ME — THE BREASTPLATE OF ST. PATRICK

I arise today through God's strength to pilot me, God's might to uphold me, God's wisdom to guide me, God's eye to look before me, God's ear to hear me, God's word to speak for me, God's hand to guard me, God's way to lie before me, God's shield to protect me.
—Saint Patrick

My new favorite protection prayer is "The Breastplate of St. Patrick":

> *Christ, be with me.*
> *Christ before me.*
> *Christ behind me.*
> *Christ in me.*
> *Christ above me.*
> *Christ beneath me.*
> *Christ on my right.*
> *Christ on my left.*
> *Christ where I lie.*
> *Christ where I sit.*
> *Christ where I arise.[1]*

Christ with me. Emmanuel. God *with* us. God *with ME*. What an impact that one word, *with*, can have on the way I envision God and how I present him to others! God *with* me—not in a general, God-is-every-where way but in a specific, right-next-to-me way. Touching me shoulder to shoulder, with his arm around me, supporting me, encouraging me, standing with me and standing up for me. He literally has my back . . . and my sides . . . and above my head . . . and below my feet. Literally.

Reading Psalm 139, I am amazed at how perfectly David captured this truth about God's surrounding us—surrounding *me*. Read this rendering from The Message slowly, and take in the nature, the heart, and the presence of the God who is right *with YOU*.

> God, investigate my life;
>> get all the facts firsthand.
> I'm an open book to you;
>> even from a distance, you know what I'm thinking.
> You know when I leave and when I get back;
>> I'm never out of your sight.
> You know everything I'm going to say
>> before I start the first sentence.
> I look behind me and you're there,
>> then up ahead and you're there, too—
>> your reassuring presence, coming and going.
> This is too much, too wonderful—
>> I can't take it all in!
> Is there anyplace I can go to avoid your Spirit?
>> to be out of your sight?
> If I climb to the sky, you're there!
>> If I go underground, you're there!
> If I flew on morning's wings
>> to the far western horizon,
> You'd find me in a minute—
>> you're already there waiting!

Then I said to myself, "Oh, he even sees me in the dark!
    At night I'm immersed in the light!"
It's a fact: darkness isn't dark to you;
    night and day, darkness and light, they're all the same to you.
Oh yes, you shaped me first inside, then out;
    you formed me in my mother's womb.
I thank you, High God—you're breathtaking!
    Body and soul, I am marvelously made!
    I worship in adoration—what a creation!
You know me inside and out,
    you know every bone in my body;
You know exactly how I was made, bit by bit,
    how I was sculpted from nothing into something.
Like an open book, you watched me grow from conception to birth;
    all the stages of my life were spread out before you,
The days of my life all prepared
    before I'd even lived one day.

There are two lines in this psalm that are either the best news we have ever heard or our worst nightmare: "I look behind me and you're there, then up ahead and you're there, too."

So, God, you are there when I am looking at the newspaper or at pornography, when I'm cheating on my taxes or helping my son with algebra, when I am waving good-bye to my spouse or gesturing to the driver who just cut me off, when I'm smoking spare ribs for dinner or smoking other things with a friend. You are there.

I do not just get God when I ask him to be with me. I get him all the time—no matter what. And no matter what, his love and mercy and grace and truth will be as constant with me as his presence. Guaranteed.

PRAYER

Father, I can hardly grasp your presence being with me all the time. I want to ponder that today. You have given me an imagination, and I want to imagine you with your arm around me. It's a position you never tire of. Thank you, Father. It is unbelievable, yet true.

THOUGHTS AND REFLECTIONS

_____

_____

_____

_____

_____

_____

_____

_____

_____

_____

_____

_____

_____

_____

_____

_____

_____

_____

_____

_____

_____

_____

_____

_____

_____

_____

_____

_____

_____

_____

_____

There is one thing that remains constant: Emmanuel, "God with us." God with me. Right alongside me. Arm around me. Always.

YOU ARE THE TREASURE OF GOD

If you want to know who you are,
you must know whose you are.
—Jerry and Denise Basel

You. It's you. *You* are the treasure of God (Mal. 3:17).

"Me. It's me. I am the treasure of God."

Read that last sentence aloud. Whisper it to yourself slowly and drink it in as deeply as you can: "I–am–the–treasure–of–God."

God desires that we not just know this in our head but also believe it matter-of-factly in our heart. He reaffirms his own heart toward us again and again in Scripture: *You are precious in my sight and I love you; I love you with an everlasting love; I rejoice over you with singing; I love you just as I love my Son, Jesus.* Yet too many of us still do not see ourselves and accept ourselves as he does. That must surely sadden him.

Let me share a story that deeply resonated with me about how God sees us. A few years ago, Jerry and I visited St. Lawrence Catholic Church outside of Atlanta. In the lobby was a display depicting a scene from one of the last days of St. Lawrence's life. Lawrence was a deacon in Rome in the fourth century—a volatile time in Rome during which the pope and several deacons had been recently martyred for their faith. Lawrence was charged with the responsibility for the material goods of the church as well as the care of the poor.

The prefect of Rome sent for Lawrence and commanded him to turn over the riches of the church to the emperor. Lawrence was granted three days to set everything in order. Three days later, Lawrence gathered a great throng of people in the courtyard—the poor, the crippled, the blind, the lepers, the orphans, and the widows. When the prefect arrived, Lawrence told him, "*These* are the treasures of the church." He was immediately taken and martyred by being roasted over hot coals.

What a profound act; what a profound statement. Lawrence "got it." He got God's heart for his people—for us. He got how God sees us. He saw that our outward appearance, our wealth, our status, our struggles, our sins—that none of these define us. Lawrence looked at the people under his care and saw God's precious children. God placed value on them. Acceptance. Inclusion. Worth. Importance. They were treasures. They did not look like treasures in the world's eyes or even to themselves. But that's how God saw them—and it's how he sees us.

I hope Lawrence, in his love for God's children, was able to help them fully grasp the astounding love of the Father for each of them—love that was demonstrated through the finished work of his Son, Jesus, on the cross. How I hope that throng of ragamuffins standing before the prefect could have shouted in unison with Lawrence, "We are the treasures of the church. We are the treasures of God."

Today, centuries later, join your heart and voice with mine. For the truth of God back then in that Roman courtyard remains the same: "We are the treasures of God."

And since God himself says we are his precious treasures, guess what? We truly are.

PRAYER

Father, help me take this truth deep within my heart. Help me see myself the way you see me, as a treasure to you. Forgive me for the times when I have been out of agreement with you on this. Your servant, Lawrence, gave his life for this truth to be made known to the people of his day. And before him, your Son, Jesus Christ, gave his life so this same truth could be made known to us for all eternity. Because of what has been done for me through him, I can with confidence proclaim, "I am the treasure of God!"

THOUGHTS AND REFLECTIONS

_____

_____

_____

_____

_____

_____

_____

_____

_____

_____

_____

_____

_____

_____

_____

_____

_____

_____

_____

_____

_____

_____

_____

_____

_____

_____

I am God's beloved. I am a jewel in his crown. I am his pearl of great price.

SEEING YOURSELF THROUGH GOD'S EYES

We are praying that we will live in the reality of these words . . . "seeing life, the world, and people, (including ourselves), using God as our glasses."
—*Frank Laubauch*

When God looks at you, what does he see? When your closest friend looks at you what, does he or she see? When you look at yourself, what do you see? Any difference among the three? What would you see if you looked at yourself again—except this time through God's glasses?

Let's take a moment to ponder the Father's thoughts and his very nature as our Creator. He has already given us a pretty clear view of how he sees us: "You are my very own handiwork, my very workmanship (Eph. 2:10). I call you by name (even your nickname) (Isa. 43:1); it is written on the palm of my hand (Isa. 49:16)."

Let me tell you a story about my own name. As a little child, I was sometimes called not Denise but Nee-see. A number of years ago, I attended a Rita Springer worship conference, where several of my clients were also in attendance. I had recently been devastated over the sudden loss of our dog, Lassie, who was like a child to me. I didn't mean to let her get so deeply into my heart, but after losing our only child to miscarriage, there was an empty place for Lassie to fill with unconditional love. Now

I was wrestling with God over whether or not I would see Lassie again in heaven. I knew I would hold my baby boy, Samuel, but would my pets be there too?

During a break for reflection, I went for a walk along the river and was asking the Father to help me with this question. After several minutes of absently staring at the water, I saw a picture in my mind of myself standing on a path in a meadow. Way down the path was a man walking with a dog. It was Jesus and Lassie. I called, "Nee-see's home." When Lassie heard my voice, she took off running to greet me. Jesus was walking behind with a huge smile on his face. This vision instantly comforted me. I just needed to know Jesus had her and I would see her again.

Now, you probably know that when you hear from God in some extrabiblical fashion, you usually have some doubt that it really was God. Maybe what I experienced was just wishful thinking or my imagination. But the next day, the weirdest thing happened. As I was leaving the conference, I was hugging my clients good-bye. One of them said, "It was nice being with you, Nee-see."

My jaw dropped. *What did she just call me?* Misinterpreting my shocked expression, the woman began to apologize, not realizing what a God moment she had opened up for me. That picture from the day before—it really was from my Father; either that, or it was the weirdest coincidence ever. But it was him. He even knew my nickname as a child.

I quickly took my client off the hook and explained to her what had happened. She was a new Christian, and discovering that God had used her in a profound way blew her mind. As God often does, he placed his kiss of affection on both of us.

At that moment, we saw ourselves through God's glasses—each of us special, chosen, worthy, his child. How often are our own thoughts toward ourselves just the opposite!

Stop and listen closely for a moment. Quiet your heart and listen to the Father's heart for you:

My child, speak of yourself as though it was me describing you. Make no room for self-hatred or self-condemnation. You are my own handiwork, made in the very image of Jesus, my Son. I have woven your identity and your destiny into the very fabric of your being. There are places I call you to go, people for you to meet, a path prepared ahead of you to walk, a place I am making ready for you to spend forever with me.

I implore you not to utter harsh words against yourself. Do you think I could ever agree with hatred toward your very self? Never. I see you as a one-of-a-kind jewel—rare and precious. Let me pick you up and polish you, removing all the stain and all the rough edges so you can shine. I am creating a new heart in you. Would you then war against your very heart? Devalue the gem of God?

I extend peace to you like a river—peace to be yourself and enjoy being yourself. To speak kindly of yourself is to humble yourself. To value yourself is to humble yourself. To be loving and gentle toward yourself is your gift to me. Look at yourself in the mirror and extend an olive branch. Give up the war with yourself. I love you. I call you with an everlasting love—constantly, constantly. If you were to think of yourself as I think of you, how different your life would be.

PRAYER

Holy Spirit, rest on me with your truth about me. It is almost too awesome to believe. You were sent to guide and dwell with me. I open the door of my heart and give you permission to nudge me when I put myself down or puff myself up. I just want to become my true self, no more or no less than you say. I get it. One more thing: When I get in trouble by thinking negative thoughts about myself, could I borrow your glasses? Thanks!

THOUGHTS AND REFLECTIONS

My Father's love for me always remains constant. It never changes—not with one good work or a thousand, not with one sin or a million.

"BUT WOULDN'T THAT BE SELFISH?"

A religion scholar . . . [tested Jesus]. "Teacher, what do
I need to do to get eternal life?" He answered,
"What's written in God's Law?
How do you interpret it?" He said, "That you love the
Lord your God with all your passion and prayer
and muscle and intelligence—and that you
love your neighbor as well as you do yourself."
"Good answer!" said Jesus. "Do it and you'll live."
—Luke 10:25–28 (MSG)

Our ability to love ourselves has a great impact on how well we love others. If learning to love myself better ultimately enables me to love *you* better, then the result is definitely not selfish. In *Waking the Dead*, John Eldredge says,

> Caring for our own hearts isn't selfishness; it's how we begin to love. Yes, we care for our hearts for the sake of others. Does that sound like a contradiction? Not at all. What will you bring to others if your heart is empty, dried up, pinned down? Love is the point. And you can't love without your heart, and you can't love well unless your heart is well.[2]

Ironically, when we do not love ourselves, we actually become more selfish. Our actions became a means to get our own needs met—needs for acceptance, security, love—instead of loving others.

Our relationship with God is also negatively affected when we don't love ourselves. By not loving ourselves, we disagree with how he sees us and feels about us. We end up actually opposing him—unintentionally, of course, but when our self-assessment becomes more important to us than the Father's assessment of us, then our actions become self-centered rather than God-centered.

Thank God there is a road out of this unhealthy place! The first step is to recognize that loving yourself as the Father loves you is not a selfish act.

PRAYER FOR THE JOURNEY

As we begin Week Two, join us as we pray:

Father, show me how you see me and how you feel about me. Help me see whether my view of myself is different from yours—if there are parts of me, parts of my very heart, that I do not love. I want to be in agreement with you. I want to love what you love. If I have felt that it was in any way wrong and selfish to look at myself this way—to love myself the way you do—I recognize that these thoughts are not from you.

Father, I trust you in this process and believe that you will guide me as I open myself to you and allow you full access to my heart.

HIDING BEHIND A MASK

God hath given you one face, and you make yourselves another.
—*William Shakespeare*

What happens when *acting* good and righteous is more important than *being* good and righteous? When acting loving is more important that being loving?

We become a human doing rather than a human being.

Taking care of others may be our means of feeling value and significance we don't otherwise experience. We may use involvement to avoid feelings of loneliness or fill a deep emptiness. We say, "I feel better about myself when I am helping. I don't want to say no and hurt someone's feelings or make things more difficult for them."

Thus, we hide what's really going on inside us. We pretend to be fine, and we say we're fine, but in reality, aren't we being dishonest? Making ourselves look good in order to get praised for it? Denying ourselves by pretending we are not feeling any emotions, even when our emotions are screaming on the inside?

"Well, it's just a little white lie." Not really—not so little and not so white. The other person has no clue and draws conclusions about us that are probably untrue: "She listened to me for over an hour and invited me to call her anytime I needed someone to talk with. She really cares about me."

We say,

"Sure we can babysit Saturday night."

"Of course you can bring your dogs."

"I can teach your Sunday school class for you this morning. No problem."

"Of course I'll be there to help decorate the church. You can always count on me."

There's nothing innately wrong with any of these things. It's good to give, good to serve others—provided our motivation is right. That's the rub: What is it that drives us? When our outwardly good actions stem from brokenness rather than wholeness, we end up lying to ourselves and avoiding our true emotions. We smile when we are sad. We laugh or lighten up around grief. We laugh when we don't think it's funny. Give compliments we don't mean. Play the game when we hate it.

We learn early on, "Don't talk. Don't feel. Don't trust." We learn to wear a mask, to project a false self and stuff down our real self—the one Christ came to heal and set free. Christ did not come to save our false self. He did not come to extend love and forgiveness to the mask. That is rubbish to him.

People may describe us as loving and caring, sacrificing and giving. And every church and family needs a few such persons around, don't they? But what if there is more to the story? What if we give love because we are starved for love ourselves? What if our selfless love is really selfish because we are giving in hopes of receiving care in return?

Can we assume all altruistic actions are authentic? In our experience as counselors, we have seen over and over that when we look under the surface of loving actions, we often find different roots and motives. A tree with branches of caring and selflessness may be fed by a root system of insecurity, hunger for attention, unmet needs for love, and longings for acceptance and belonging.

When we cannot say no for fear of not being liked . . .
When we give because the person next to us is giving, and we don't want
to look bad . . .

When we resent that others aren't doing their fair share, yet we say, "Oh, that's okay, I'll finish up. You go on home."...
When we smile on the outside but feel used on the inside...

... then at the very core of our altruism is a wound—a cry for love, affection, and belonging: needs that were not met in our formative years and now lie hidden behind our false self. Behind our mask.

And unfortunately, as one leader has put it, "It's the mask that gets the love." So the hole in our soul never gets healed, our cry never gets heard, and our emptiness keeps growing.

We all must come to the place of accepting that the holes and broken places in our lives originated in our formative years. We may try to work on self-improvement, learn new things, or try harder to be a better person or even a better Christian. We may do more "Christian" things. But our core pain and unhealthy patterns will not be addressed by looking better on the outside. Like the Pharisees, we'll be focusing on the outside of our cup while remaining full of dead bones on the inside (Matt. 23:25). The Pharisees were told to turn their hearts inside out to expose the real problem. That's what we have to do as well.

Are you willing to go on this journey into the feared and the unknown? To find out where you abandoned yourself? Where your feelings got stuffed or deadened? Where you became a doer rather than a be-er? Where you had to look good to please others and feel better about yourself? Where your real feelings, thoughts, and beliefs could not be expressed? Where you started to project a false front so you would be liked and appreciated? Where you became overly responsible, concerned for others rather than yourself? Where you became a rescuer and fixer? Where you became fearful of criticism yet were overly critical toward yourself? Where you began to feel alone even when you were around others?

We can bet that most people around you would never have a clue. Why? Because they only see the mask—the public self—and honestly, they have never met who you are. And neither have you.

PRAYER

Father, I need your help to find my true self. I want to be honest with you and with myself, so I can then be honest with others. Even when I have been applauded for my performance, perfection, or commitment, the praise has gone to my false self. I want the love and acceptance of others to go to my true self instead of the image I portray.

Lord, I am tired. I am tired of performing. Tired of feeling like a phony. I confess that I cannot keep all the plates spinning anymore. I need you—all of you. I've heard stories about your healing the brokenhearted and setting the captives free. And because you are always honest about everything you say, I trust you. Here I am, Lord. I'm ready for you to do the unveiling so I can meet the real me.

THOUGHTS AND REFLECTIONS

When I lose who I am in order to please others, I don't have a self to truly give away.

MOMENTS OF GOD'S REVEALED LOVE

*What he is after is us—our laughter, our tears, our dreams,
our fears, our heart of hearts. How few of us truly believe this.
We've never been wanted for our heart, our truest self, not
really, not for long. The thought that God wants
our heart seems too good to be true.*
–John Eldredge

Two stories come to mind when I think of God's unfailing love for his children. One is of a grandmother speaking to her troubled grandson. The other is of a young college woman undone by the words of her professor.

It tenderizes my heart when I see how God breaks in and leaves his permanent fingerprint on our hearts. These moments change us and encourage us to stay on the journey God has for us.

Almost every day, Jerry and I and our border collie, Grace, take a walk up the mountain where we live. One day, a precious lady stopped her car to talk to us. She asked us to pray for her twenty-year-old grandson, who had been in and out of treatment for drug addiction. She told us, "I put my hands on the side of his face and looked him right in his eyes. I told him that I hurt for him because of his struggle. I told him I would never stop praying for him—never give up on him—that I would never stop loving him completely—no matter what."

We were undone by her beautiful reflection of the Father's love to her grandson. We couldn't help thinking, "If she can love her grandson that deeply and unwaveringly, how much more and more and more does the Father love us?"

A young college woman sent us this letter sharing how God broke into her heart:

> I am feeling so affirmed in who I am as a daughter of God. I had a unique moment as I sat in class the day after I got back from my ministry time with you. My professor, so full of life and love, was talking about sharing with his children their significance in the eyes of God. He was describing that they are home-schooled and that they struggle with mathematics. He told the class, "Whenever my children are struggling with a subject in school I say to them tenderly, 'How many math problems do you have to get right for Jesus to love you? — NONE! You are loved by God and are significant to him, not because of what you do but because you were made by him, and he just loves you because you are YOU!'"
>
> My eyes filled with tears as my teacher spoke to us. It felt like he was speaking to me as his child. I was able to receive something then that I never experienced with my own father. It was a powerful, powerful moment for me. In that moment, it was almost as if my teacher was a surrogate father and I felt like I was receiving his message when I was eight years old. For the first time in my life, I felt in my HEART—not just in my head—that I was significant to God. For so long I have KNOWN this truth, but have not FELT this truth.
>
> The Lord is also beginning to undo a pattern of people pleasing and burden bearing in my life. I have begun to understand that I take on the burdens of others—ones that I am not supposed to carry. I know that the Lord has much more to reveal to me in this area, but I feel as if I have been set on the right path. I am excited for the journey ahead as I continue to walk in freedom and to grow in my identity in Christ.

In these stories, both the grandmother and the professor revealed the Father's heart of love, acceptance, and compassion for his children. Each person extended God's arms to someone in need, and in so doing, demonstrated to all of us our call to be God's light to a broken and hurting world.

PRAYER

Father, I know in my head that your love for me is unconditional, but it is still working its way into my heart. How could it be that no matter what I do, you will never, ever stop loving me? Take me deeper into your heart and help me feel the reality of this truth—that your love for me is complete and non-changing. How my life will be different when this gets deeper into my heart! How much more will I love you, myself, and others with this revelation! So have your way and help me to know and experience your revealed love for me.

THOUGHTS AND REFLECTIONS

When I become my true child-of-God self, I will be able to reflect his love and acceptance toward myself and others.

ASSUMPTIONS

We are created by love, to live in love, for the sake of love.
—Gerald May

An *assumption* is a "no-brainer," a supposition assumed to be true without proof, something that is taken for granted. There are three Scriptures in the gospel of Matthew that make assumptions. The first is in Matthew 6:12—the Lord's Prayer.

When I was a child, the members at my church all joined in to pray the Lord's Prayer. I used to look around at them and wonder why everyone found that prayer so easy to pray—particularly when we were asking God to forgive us just as we forgave those who had hurt us, wronged us, broken us, sinned against us, offended us, rejected us. I wanted to shout out, "Really, people? You actually want God to forgive you exactly the same way you forgive others?" I knew these people, and many of them "forgave" by getting even, cutting others off, cursing them, giving them the silent treatment, gossiping about them, criticizing them, judging them, and justifying their anger toward them.

I hope God is more merciful to me than I am to others and to myself. And the great news is that he is, because he can't deny his own nature—he is love.

We find two other assumptions of Scripture in Matthew 22:37–39. The first involves the Great Commandment: "Love the Lord your God."

How? "With all your heart, soul, mind and strength." In other words, with all you've got, nothing held back—with everything.

First assumption: When we love the Lord, we can take for granted that we are to do so with all of our heart. But Jesus says there is a second command that hangs right next to the first: "Love your neighbor." How? "As much as you love yourself."

And that leads us to our second assumption: If we are to love others as we love ourselves, then it seems Jesus is saying that loving ourselves is something else we can take for granted—as if everyone loves (and likes) themselves. Jesus actually uses it as the standard so we can know how much we need to love others.

So ponder this: How do you think God feels when his children, whom he personally created, do not like themselves or love themselves; when they criticize themselves, reject themselves, harm themselves, or curse themselves? I think that just as you would want to encourage and affirm a child who was down on himself, our Father longs to do the same for us, except perfectly.

Stop for a moment and feel his deep longing that you would see what he sees when he looks at you, feel what he feels in his heart toward you. It may seem wrong to believe what he says about you—even a little prideful and arrogant. But what God says is true no matter what you think or whether you agree with him. After all, he designed you, and you are not damaged goods. His primary focus is to draw you lovingly back into the truth about who you are.

And that truth, the truth of how much he loves you, is a perfect place for another assumption: There is nothing you can ever do to make God love you less. And right alongside it hangs another assumption like it: There is nothing you can ever do to make God love you more. That is how God loves—and that's the truth. A no-brainer.

PRAYER

Father, how gracious of you to always assume the best about me, believe in me, and cheer me on. It is quite overwhelming to think how vast your heart for me is. How can I hold so much love in this broken vessel?

Thank you that you give me grace for the journey—grace to grow and become more of who you made me to be. I know there will be pain and sorrows to bear. I know you will stretch me along the way. Help me know that the stretching will enlarge my heart's capacity to love. And love is at the center of the greatest commandments. Love God. Love self (so I have something that can overflow onto others). Then love others. A perfect circle.

THOUGHTS AND REFLECTIONS

_____

_____

_____

_____

_____

_____

_____

_____

_____

_____

_____

_____

_____

_____

_____

_____

_____

_____

_____

_____

_____

_____

_____

_____

_____

_____

It is impossible for me to do a good job of keeping the first commandment, loving God, without fulfilling all of the second.

IS IT UNSCRIPTURAL TO LOVE MYSELF?

*Of all the people you will know in a lifetime,
you are the only one you will never leave or lose.*
—*Jo Coudart*

Recently we were confronted by a Christian leader who believes loving yourself is not only selfish but also unscriptural. Pondering the matter today, I (Denise) worked through the love chapter, 1 Corinthians 13, as my grid for what love is supposed to look like. I came up with an if/then hypothesis: *If* Scripture says this about love, and I believe I am not to "love myself," *then* I should . . ." Filling in the blank for each item the apostle Paul listed, I arrived at the following:

- *Love is patient.* So if I am to love others and not myself, then as an obedient Christ-follower, presumably I should be testy, impatient, and intolerant with myself. *Really? Is that what my Father wants for me?*
- *Love is kind.* So should I be unkind to myself, critical, and even cruel? Whatever is the opposite of being kind, is that how I should treat myself?
- *Love honors others.* So should I dishonor and discredit myself, put myself down and demean myself? (Teenagers are experts at this. Should we encourage them to hate themselves even more?)

How difficult is it to be around someone who is self-condemning, self-deprecating, and self-judging—and have you ever wondered whether that describes yourself?

- *Love is not self-seeking.* So does that mean that I should have no voice, no opinion, and no desire that should be considered? Is it okay to let people walk all over me, control me, use me, and abuse me? Is it ideal to have a church full of Christian doormats who have no boundaries?

- *Love is not easily angered.* I guess without self-love, it would be good and right to beat myself up for the smallest things. Does that make me more Christ-like?

- *Love keeps no record of wrongs.* I'm to forgive others, but when it comes to myself, the godly thing is for me to keep a running tally of self-accusations, mistakes, and failures—basically my entire I-don't-measure-up list. Have I got that right?

- *Love always protects.* Heaven forbid I should protect myself. What is there that is worth protecting?

- *Love always trusts.* So to be godly, am I to distrust myself—the very person God fashioned me to be in my mother's womb? If so, how do I go about making decisions for my daily life?

- *Love always hopes.* Is it wrong, then, for me to hope for my future, for peace in my heart, and for growth in my character and my faith?

- *Love always perseveres.* Does that mean I should be a quitter and give up on myself? Does that sound like something the Father desires for me?

I guess 1 Corinthians 13 needs to be modified to read something like this: "Be impatient, unkind, dishonoring, critical, and unforgiving toward yourself. Don't protect yourself or stand up for yourself; don't hope for yourself or believe in yourself."

But if we are not to love ourselves, then why would the Father send his only Son to save us? The answer is, he wouldn't. The very fact that he did is proof that we have value, that we are special and precious in his sight. He is our Father and we are his children. We are the very bearers of his glory and his Spirit. The Father I know longs to heal his children of the struggles and lies that hurt and degrade them. Only when I love myself as God's own child can I truly love others with the same love and acceptance he pours into me.

God himself has called us worthy and chosen—and definitely worth loving.

PRAYER

Father, I need to hold 1 Corinthians 13 as an overlay upon my own life. Holy Spirit, guide me to truly love others more by first learning to love myself. I believe that as I become more forgiving of myself, I will be more forgiving of others. That as I am more grace-filled toward myself, I will more readily extend grace to others. As I am more encouraging, trusting, patient, kind, and honoring of myself, others will see a reflection of your love in my eyes. Father, help me to love myself the way you do: Completely. Unswervingly. Unfailingly.

THOUGHTS AND REFLECTIONS

_____

_____

_____

_____

_____

_____

_____

_____

_____

_____

_____

_____

_____

_____

_____

_____

_____

_____

_____

_____

_____

_____

_____

_____

_____

_____

Ironically, when we do not love ourselves, we actually become more selfish.

THE PRICE OF NOT DOING ANGER

The church has very efficiently pared the claws of the Lion of Judah, making him a fitting household pet for pale curates and pious old ladies. Is that the God you find in the Bible?
—John Eldredge

A common theme that shows up with many of the counselees we work with is to "avoid anger at all cost." I (Jerry) know this one really well, because I lived the first thirty-six years of my life with this belief. I was "imprinted" by growing up in a home where anger was commonly present—from my father—and I decided I didn't want anything to do with that emotion. As we do with so many of our responses to things we don't like or that have been hurtful to us, I decided that all anger was damaging and hurtful. I would *not* have it!

Since I saw the unhealthy and sinful expressions of anger, I never realized that *not* expressing anger was also unhealthy. It never dawned on me that I needed anger. I didn't realize that anger didn't have to be my enemy and could actually be a friend. This revelation came to me when I started pursuing my emotional healing at around thirty-six years old.

What is the problem with avoiding anger? Doing so stops us from living. Anger says that something matters—that *I* matter. Anger can tell us something is wrong, and it may involve our seeing that it's made right.

Anger typically is just a pointer to something deeper—pain, fear, or loss—and if we allow anger to do its work, then that wound can be identified and addressed.

Some time ago, one of our clients came to realize how damaging it had been for him to never feel and express anger. He wrote down some of the ways denying his anger had negatively impacted his life. He called it "The Price I Paid Because I Don't Feel Anger." Here are a few of the ways he identified:

- It keeps me from pursuing a full life. I don't reveal my heart.
- I am not authentic.
- I am robbing my relationships. I don't build bridges. I am not transparent.
- My passions and desires go unmet.
- It keeps me in an "I don't matter" way of thinking.
- I don't expose (or reveal) what I value.
- I don't tell the truth.
- I don't validate my experiences.
- I ignore the warning signals that tell me to look inside at deeper issues.
- I don't take responsibility for my feelings and identify them.
- I don't have the guts to confess, admit, or show up.
- I don't expose (or reveal) my choices and truths.
- No one knows what matters to me because I don't commit to what matters.

Like this client, I myself was unable (and unwilling) to acknowledge and express anger in a healthy manner, so a part of me remained hidden—to myself and to others. Denise didn't have all of my heart, and God surely didn't either. I had built walls around it and didn't even know it.

So what do you do when you realize you've shut down and avoided expressing anger? First, you acknowledge that you made an internal decision that was not in agreement with what God says about anger (see examples of Jesus's expression of anger in Mark 3:1–6 and John 2:15–17), and you ask him to allow you to feel it. When the feelings of anger start to come, there must also be a way to begin to communicate them. It initially may involve writing them down on paper. In many cases, when the submerged anger begins to surface, feelings of hurt, pain, and grief will surface as well. As you allow these to come up, the walls around your heart will start to come down.

Beginning to risk and share some of these feelings with someone close to you who is trustworthy is also very important. But remember: although you'll never want to intentionally hurt another person by expressing your anger and associated feelings, you undoubtedly *will* hurt someone close to you. You will make mistakes. What then? Shut down your anger again? NO. Run to God, acknowledge the mistake, and then run back to the one you've hurt and apologize. You must continue to risk vulnerability in this new area of living.

I am so glad I became aware many years ago of how I had shut down anger and how doing so had impacted others and me. As a result of owning my anger and dealing with it in a healthy way, I'm not the same person I was back then—and that's a good thing.

PRAYER

Lord Jesus, I want to feel what you felt when you walked this earth and what you still feel today. You felt anger and yet did not sin. It is possible for me to learn to do that as well. I invite you to open up my heart and allow me to feel the full range of emotions. I know that if I shut down any particular emotion, then I shut down a part of my heart, and I don't want that. So I trust you with my heart and all of my feelings—including anger—and I ask you to have your way.

THOUGHTS AND REFLECTIONS

_____
_____
_____
_____
_____
_____
_____
_____
_____
_____
_____
_____
_____
_____
_____
_____
_____
_____
_____
_____
_____
_____
_____
_____
_____
_____

Authentic anger is a passionate feeling which tells us that something matters —and our emotions matter. Anger is often what guides us to the source of our pain, where the Father desires to bring healing.

COME AS A CHILD

Consider the incredible love that the Father has shown us in allowing us to be called "children of God"—and that is not just what we are called, but what we are.
—1 John 3:1 (Phillips)

Of all the Scriptures the Father has emphasized in our healing ministry, some of the most profound have related to coming to him as a child. No matter how old we get, the Father still refers to us as children. He adopts us as his own, and even if we surrender our lives to God at seventy years of age, we are to come as a child.

Jesus was very clear on his position regarding children and the kingdom of God. Remember that when we see Jesus, we see the Father (John 14:9). During the ministry of Jesus, he only did what his Father was doing (John 5:19)—and one of the things Jesus made a point of doing was to welcome little children (Mark 10:13–16). So when Jesus expresses the importance of children and childlikeness, it is because they are dear to the very heart of God.

PRAYER FOR THE JOURNEY

As we begin Week Three, pray with us:

Jesus, your ministry here on earth made a place for children. Your heart was, and still is, turned toward them. I invite you to show me more about the child within me. Is my own heart turned toward that child? Do I embrace this child like you do? Or would I rather, like your disciples, shoo the child away because there are more important things to attend to? Do I, like a child, engage in the wonder and joy of your creation?

Jesus, you reveal your Father's heart. I want my heart to be in agreement with you and your Father about the child inside me. I want to be healed and whole—every part of me—and I invite you to reveal where this child was wounded and bring your healing love to those places.

Please also show me where my picture of you has been distorted, and help me to see you and your heart clearly and truly. By your grace, I will embrace my child within and bring that part of me to you. I trust you in this.

YOU'RE JUST LIKE YOUR FATHER

You teach what you know,
But you impart who you are.
—Jack Frost

Jesus came to point us to the Father. If you have seen Jesus, you have seen the Father (John 14:9). If you've known Jesus's compassion, love, forgiveness, tenderness, and tears, then you know Abba Father's as well. If you know his teaching, leading, guiding, correcting, and healing—then, you also know Abba Father's. The heart of Jesus and the Father are identical. Jesus wants everyone to know that if you overlay his attributes right on top of the Father's, it would be a perfect match.

Sometimes in our Christianity, we choose to focus primarily on Jesus (our salvation through the cross) and pray only to Jesus. Is it okay to love and pray to Jesus and keep our distance from the Father? It's amazing to us how many people can pray to God in general, but when we ask them to pray, "Father God," they cannot because of the overlay of their earthly fathers onto God. As counselors, we know that the disconnect or resistance to the Father is usually from a childhood wound.

A client of ours who had been sexually abused by her father had to wrestle for a year over her repulsion of God as Father. It wasn't that she hated God; she just couldn't punch through the image of her abusive father. With painstaking slowness, God pulled back the layers of her wounds and healed her.

Sometimes the words "You're just like your father/mother" can be flattering. For instance: "You have your father's wit—his charm—his business sense," or, "You have your mother's creativity—her musical ability—her warm personality." But in our counseling experience, being compared to one's parent is rarely a compliment.

Let's say you told all your friends or even your own children, "When you see me, you've seen my father (or mother). I am just like him/her." I don't know about you, but I know several people who would cringe at that statement. During a heated argument, spouses may use words like that as a weapon. Things seldom go well after that; it is definitely not taken as a compliment. In counseling, we ask couples to make a covenant with each other to never say "You're just like . . ."; it just adds fuel to the fire.

When a spouse throws the dagger, "You are just like your father (or mother)," it often communicates something specific. Ponder each statement below and see which ones describe your father or mother when you were growing up. Then ask yourself if any of these issues show up in your significant relationships.

- You are not there for us when we need you. You are always working or watching sports—just like your father.
- You never make time for the kids or me. We don't matter. If you didn't bring home the paycheck, we wouldn't even know you live here—just like your father.
- You are so selfish. Everything is always about you—just like your mother.
- You always tell other people what to do, but nobody can tell you anything. You are so stubborn—just like your mother.
- You never admit you're wrong and don't even believe you ever are. You never say you're sorry—just like your father.
- You never tell the kids you love them and are proud of them just for who they are—just like your father.

- You never show any emotions except anger and rage—just like your father.
- You are controlling. Mean. Perfectionistic. Critical. Abusive. Rigid. Explosive. Selfish—just like your mother.
- You shame us with your words, gestures, or even just a look. You send a message that we can never measure up—just like your mother.
- You are passive, unloving, uncaring, uninvolved. You are absent —just like your mother.

Whether we like it or not, the wounds from our parents direct future patterns and ways we relate to others, especially in our closest relationships. We have heard so many people say they vowed never to be like their father or mother; then, to their chagrin, they became like their parent in more ways than they wanted to admit. We may attempt to tweak ourselves a little so it seems we're not like our parents. But as the saying goes, "If it looks like a duck, walks like a duck, and quacks like a duck, then it's a duck."

What patterns do you see in yourself that have an origin in your childhood? Does it even matter? Yes! It unequivocally matters to the Father. Your past is a place he longs to heal. Let him search your heart, showing you the rooms he wants to open and expose to the light of his truth. Follow him from room to room, and allow him to begin healing all your brokenness and redeem your past. Your life. Only then will you be empowered to consistently respond—not merely react—in a healthy way.

Determine today to stop the generational patterns in yourself and in your children. The Father is all about helping you do that, so you can be more like him. He is hoping that the next time someone says to you, "You are just like your Father," you can say, "Thanks."

Thank God there is a road out of unhealthiness to wholeness. The first step is to recognize that loving yourself as the Father loves you is not a selfish act. Rather, to do otherwise is to disagree with the Father—and the Father is always right.

PRAYER

Father, this healing journey is taking longer than I thought. I thought that once I let you build the house in me, we would be finished—that you and I could just get on with doing life. But I can see that if you simply fixed me, I could get ahead of you instead of surrendering in utter dependence. Thank you, Father, that when I lean on you, you will never, and can never, move away—because you are always with me.

Help me again and again to come as a child, needing your strength in my weakness; your hope in my despair; your comfort for my pain, my fear, and my grief; your light when I am surrounded by darkness; your unchangeable presence when I feel rejected and alone. Loving Father, give me your eyes to see, your ears to hear, and your heart to understand—me. More of you in me makes me "just like my Father." Thanks.

THOUGHTS AND REFLECTIONS

_____

_____

_____

_____

_____

_____

_____

_____

_____

_____

_____

_____

_____

_____

_____

_____

_____

_____

_____

_____

_____

_____

_____

_____

_____

_____

_____

_____

The heart of God is to heal each generation that invites him to do so. We do not believe that the subsequent generations are destined to repeat and relive the wounding from the past.

GO GIVE GRANDMA
A HUG

It's weird. You got to figure this out to be a grown-up. But once
you become one, you got to turn right around and be more
like a kid again. Doesn't that strike you as strange? It does me.
Like you got to be both when you can't be but one. It's tricky.
Anyway, that's what I think.
—Charles Martin

Remember visiting relatives as a kid and being told to "go give Grandma and Grandpa (or your aunt or uncle) a hug"? I never liked that part. Shy as a child and afraid of adults, I (Denise) felt most comfortable sitting in the background somewhere and listening to grown-ups joking and bantering. I liked being on the outside looking in—I felt safe there. It's sad when I think of it.

Many children are given the message that they're "to be seen and not heard." I was one of them. Yet inside, I was still hoping to be noticed enough for my grandpa to offer me a bowl of maple nut ice cream or for my aunt to offer me candy from her huge candy jar. Since I was afraid to ask either of them, I would instead ask my mom if I could have some ice cream, candy, a cookie, or whatever. Rather than whispering back, she would say out loud for all to hear, "Well, go ahead and ask Grandpa if you can have some." Busted. Exposed. Shamed. Yes, especially shamed. Better for me if I didn't have needs or wants. Of course, when I asked, the answer was always yes, but it still never stopped me from wishing that the next time the treat would just be offered as an overflow of care and love for me.

I love this story from one of our clients:

> A little boy goes with his parents to visit his aunt. The little boy says, "Aunt Millie, can I have a cookie?" His mother shushes him and says, "Honey, you need to wait for someone to offer you something to eat." The little boy gets quiet for a moment. Then he looks at his aunt and says, "Aunt Millie, could you offer me a cookie?"

I like how Jesus modeled the importance of children for us. He was the one who initiated gathering the children to himself, laying his hands on each one, and blessing them individually. As Jesus did with the children that day, that's how I'd have liked to be treated—for someone to have come to me and given me a bear hug, or a kiss on the forehead, or a cookie. I would have liked the adult to be the first to show approval and love. It sure would have felt better to return hugs rather than having to initiate them.

Do you think we may have some of these rules of etiquette mixed up? As adults, are we not the ones who should demonstrate love, care, acceptance and affection to the child first? Isn't our love and acceptance what we really need children to internalize so they can model love and acceptance when they grow up? Or do we need them to be little grown-ups so the parents can feel better about themselves because they have such nice, polite children who don't embarrass the family?

In Mark 10:13–16, the disciples seemed to think the children were a bother to Jesus, less important, a nuisance to just shoo away. Jesus shocked them with his irate response. Ponder each of the following statements separately and grasp Jesus's heart:

> "Don't push these children away.
> Don't *ever* get between them and me.

These children are at the *very center* of life in the kingdom.
Mark this [pay attention]: Unless you accept God's kingdom *in the simplicity of a child*, you'll *never* get in." (MSG, emphases ours).

Then he modeled for them what he meant by gathering the children up in his arms and laying his hands of blessing on each one.

The way I see it, when I get to heaven, no one will be telling me to go give Jesus a hug. He will already be hugging me before anyone says a word. That's the kingdom.

PRAYER

Jesus, thank you that you modeled love for us—that your very essence is love. As one of your children, I thank you that you aren't far off, waiting for me to find you and come to you to receive your love. You are the true representative of your Father—the God who runs to us (Luke 15). You also tell us that we can run to the throne of grace—to you—and find help in our time of need. So even when I want to come and give you a hug, you have already placed that desire in my heart. Thank you for your love and for your hugs!

THOUGHTS AND REFLECTIONS

_____

_____

_____

_____

_____

_____

_____

_____

_____

_____

_____

_____

_____

_____

_____

_____

_____

_____

_____

_____

_____

_____

_____

_____

_____

_____

_____

Children don't understand that when their parents withhold affection and affirmation or inflict any type of abuse, it reveals something sadly missing in the parents, not something hopelessly flawed in the child.

DANCING ON DADDY'S SHOES

Jesus wants us to become like children because our spirits live closest to the surface during childhood. In childhood our hearts are the most transparent, most vulnerable, most malleable. God wants us to become the person we really are inside, the person we were born to be. Becoming childlike involves peeling away the masks to get back to the real, rosy-cheeked, bright-eyed face beneath.
—Mike Mason

When I (Denise) was growing up, polka music was part of family life. We woke up to polkas every weekend morning (no sleeping in for us), because my dad always turned up the volume loud to serve as an alarm clock. Polkas had fun lyrics for kids, like "You can't dance the polka with beans in your ears," or "Hoopi shoopi, Donna," or "Now's the time to roll the barrel, for the gang's all here." The polka "Who Stole the Kishka?" was an all-time favorite. Even now, when the songs start playing in my head, they automatically spill out of my mouth (much to Jerry's chagrin).

The very best time for polka music was at weddings. My dad could dance around the floor with the best of them. It was a special moment when he took me out on the dance floor with him. We twirled and spun so fast I would get dizzy, but I never tripped or missed a step, because I was either standing on Daddy's shoes or flying with my feet off the floor. I think every kid would love that—laughing and feeling safe in Daddy's arms.

My dad was a lot like my heavenly Father—they both like to lead the dance. When Father God leads, we learn to lean into him. We learn to hang on tight and trust. He has us. He will never let us go. He knows the next dance step in our life, and I am pretty sure it is not as predictable as one-two-three, one-two-three. It's more like one-two-three, two-five-one, nine-six-eight, three-seven-four. You get the picture.

The many mysteries about God are sometimes frustrating because we long to understand the "whys" of life. But one aspect of God remains totally predictable and constant. It's his love—his heart. That never changes, not even a little bit. In his *ways*, however, he is totally *unpredictable*. That's where our trust is put to the test—where we have to listen for the "beat" of our Creator and discover the rhythm we can move to, one step at a time.

I can hear him ask, "Can I have this dance?" When I say yes, it becomes imperative for me to surrender to his lead and lean fully into him in dependence. I become once again like a child who trusts Daddy in the dance.

PRAYER

Father, take my hand. You are the Lord of the dance. Lead me through today, and help me lean into you and trust you again tomorrow. I surrender my self-reliance and my independence, and I exchange them for dependence on you. Help me learn that leaning on you is the only position I need. Take me places where my feet never touch the floor, and let me find myself once again dancing on Daddy's shoes.

THOUGHTS AND REFLECTIONS

No matter how old we get, the Father still refers to us as children.

FROM ORPHAN TO SONSHIP

I will not leave you as orphans;
I will come to you.
—*Jesus Christ (John 14:18)*

Can you be an orphan without having been given away by your birth parents? In the legal and physical senses, no. But can you live your life as though you are an orphan? Absolutely. I (Jerry) know because, while I was never given up by my birth parents, I nevertheless lived for many years with what we and others have termed an *orphan heart* or *orphan spirit.*

One way to view this condition is to come at it from the opposite direction. If I am *not* an orphan, then I am a son of my birth parents, and I belong to that family. And being my parents' son will, by definition, identify me as having the state of sonship in that relationship.

But sonship means so much more than simply existing as a son (or daughter) by birth. It means that I not only *know* I am a son, but that I *experience* that reality in my soul and spirit. It is not just my *position*; it is also my *condition*—how I live. (In the Bible, sonship is inclusive of males and females).

Having an orphan heart has to do with whether we function more as a servant or as a son or daughter, a cherished family member or an employee or hired hand.

How about you? Do you experience God as a loving Father or more like one who is a master whom you must please? Can you feel secure in who you are and thus operate from a place of rest and peace, or do you struggle with insecurities and find it difficult to relax? Do you strive for the praise, approval, and acceptance of people and God (even if you keep it under wraps), or do you feel fully accepted in God's love and justified by his grace?

Are you independent and self-reliant, or can you acknowledge your needs and easily receive help from others? Do you find it hard to receive constructive criticism? Do you become defensive and struggle with needing to be right? These are just a few sample questions. If you connect more with the negative aspects, it is possible that you are operating more as a servant than a son or daughter of God.

What's wrong with being a servant? Doesn't Christ himself say that "'whoever wants to become great among you . . . must be slave of all'" (Mark 10:43–44)? He does indeed. But in another place, Paul writes that "the Spirit you received does not make you slaves, so that you live in fear again; rather, the Spirit you received brought about your adoption to sonship. And by him we cry, '*Abba,* Father'" (Rom. 8:15).

The issue here is function versus identity. If I do not know that I have been adopted into the position of sonship, I will work to prove my worth and value to my master. That is what a servant does when he has been hired to fulfill his role. Though he may be a good servant, he has no permanent security in that role. If his master decides to release him from his position, that is what will happen. Thus a servant can never rest fully secure.

But the person who has been adopted into a family through the actions of the parents knows who and whose he is and where he belongs. Those issues are settled, legally and spiritually, so there is rest. Security as a son or daughter removes fear from the equation. It is from *that* identity that a person can serve his master, Jesus, and others as well—not because he has to but because he *desires* to.

This is the reality that occurs—and which we are to experience—when we become children of God through placing our faith in his Son, Jesus Christ. From this position, we will never hear the words "You're fired."

I knew that my father and mother loved me as a child and throughout my life. However, there were things that happened to me that should not have happened and things that didn't happen that needed to happen. That created what are called *love deficits* within me. And in those deep places, I began to operate more from fear and anxiety and less from love and security.

Not until I was in my mid-thirties and had submitted my life to Christ did I realize the depth of my wounds. It took the love of God through Christ to open up my heart and allow me to see and experience how much I was operating from an orphaned heart. I had to trust God to bring healing to these orphaned places so I could find greater peace in my relationship with him and others.

In counseling many believing men and women, we have been grieved to see how few of them grasp the personal significance of adoption into sonship. Instead, the relationship with God becomes "Just tell me what to do and I'll do it." That is not relational at all! Can you imagine having that kind of arrangement with your spouse or friends? It is *not* the relationship Jesus modeled with his Father, and it is *not* what he wants us to have with him.

Have you been operating from more of an orphan heart than a heart of sonship? If your answer is yes, start by acknowledging your orphaned condition and ask God to begin transforming it. Ask him to reveal how your heart ended up like this. Usually the problem tracks back to some love deficits in childhood. Begin to reject the lies upon which your orphan heart started to form, and start to embrace your true identity— the one God breathed into your spirit from the very beginning of your life. Invite God into those places of pain, and let him grieve with you regarding the cost you have paid.

Eventually you will be enabled to forgive those who need to be forgiven, and God can restore your heart to the fullness of the identity that is yours by inheritance.

PRAYER

Father, thank you for adopting me into your family. Thank you that I have the spirit of sonship and am not an orphan. Yet I still struggle with living from an orphan heart. I want to securely rest in my identity as your child. I invite you to come and show me the root of my sense of not belonging. I know that when you reveal areas that need your healing love, you will bring that healing to me.

I also know that there may be grief connected with the feelings of not fully belonging. I am willing to grieve as you allow me to. Just be with me. I know you also grieve for your children's pain, and you grieve for and with me. Thank you that you will never allow me to live with an orphan heart if I truly want it to change. Thank you for the grace to change and find life— more life—with you.

THOUGHTS AND REFLECTIONS

_____
_____
_____
_____
_____
_____
_____
_____
_____
_____
_____
_____
_____
_____
_____
_____
_____
_____
_____
_____
_____
_____
_____
_____
_____

When we choose sonship, the miracle of grace becomes actualized in our heart the way God intended.

REVIVAL OF THE INNER CHILD

I have always wondered what Jesus really meant by his ultimatum to "come as a child." Your book was the doorway that opened my understanding. . . . I now have a hidden treasure living right inside me. I am no longer just a worshipper—I am a "free" worshipper. And coming as a little child, simple and trusting, has made all the difference.
—Men's Group Leader

Recently, while preparing to teach a two-day conference, I (Denise) came across a story from Christian counselor Julianne Maki. She told of hearing a prophetic message that a revival of unprecedented proportions would begin soon, starting with the children. The word stirred inside her powerfully, and it had a personal twist. Julianne wrote,

> The Lord immediately reminded me that I needed to become more in touch with the spontaneous, feeling child within me and that *my own revival* would come through that child. In fact, I believe that if the church "became as little children," then we would see the Kingdom of God come in much greater power than we have yet. Revival needs to begin with the child in each of us.[3]

Jerry and I gave our lives to Christ when we were thirty-three. We set out to live our best years yet with the Father, Son, and Holy Spirit walking with us. But God gave us a one-year grace period and then started messing with us. The next thing we knew, God came to a dead stop in his walk with us, turned around, and started heading back to our past.

Really, God? Seriously? We were having so much fun growing in the newness of you. There was still that new car smell. It never occurred to us that he would want to heal our entire lives—all the way back to our conception. You see, we were not just thirty-somethings to him. We were also newborns, toddlers, first graders, ten-year-olds, sixteen-year-olds . . . Every day of our lives makes up who we are, and Jesus came to heal and save all of us at every age.

Some Bible translations state that we must be "converted" and become like little children. That means we must change from one form into another. In that transaction, all of life is changed; old things pass away, and all things become new (2 Cor. 5:17). It is a dramatic and life-altering transformation that secures our eternal destiny. Obviously it is critically important. Yet Jesus places the same importance on receiving the kingdom of God like a little child. He says if we don't enter the kingdom in this way, we will never enter it at all. Period.

Jesus is not using the phrase "like a little child" as simply a metaphor or illustration. He actually brought a little child in front of the crowd to demonstrate his point and told them they must become *just like* that child. Ponder this passage in Matthew 18:2–4 in The Message:

> Jesus called over a child, whom he stood in the middle of the room, and said, "I'm telling you, once and for all, that unless you return to square one and start over like children, you're not even going to get a look at the kingdom, let alone get in. Whoever becomes simple and elemental again, like this child, will rank high in God's kingdom."

What do you think they saw when they looked closely at that little child standing next to Jesus? What would *you* see? Someone who is to be seen and not heard? Hardly. Just another mouth to feed? Never. Someone to shoo away because they are less important? No—heaven forbid.

Remember how irate Jesus was toward his disciples for pushing aside the little children? When he said, "'If anyone causes one of these little ones—those who believe in me—to stumble, it would be better for them to have a large millstone hung around their neck and to be drowned in the depths of the sea'" (Matt. 18:6), I hope the crowd was speechless and in wonder at Jesus's words. I hope they wondered what kind of God and Father and Savior desires us to become like children, with a childlikeness that never strives to grow up and be somebody, because we know we already *are* somebody. Doesn't that take a load of performance off us right there?

In counseling adults, we've seen how greatly God desires to take every person back to heal the past—the child within. It makes sense, doesn't it, that God would want to resurrect the parts of us that look more alive, fresh, spontaneous, curious? The child who is a bundle of energy and just exudes life? The child who is dependent and needs God and others? Contrast that child with the adult us: We're more head and less heart (feelings). More uptight, calculating, guarded, and controlling. More performance based and less free to be seen, less free to just *be*.

Step back and look at the two descriptions side by side. Can you understand more clearly why Jesus said, "I assure you *and* most solemnly say to you, unless you repent [that is, change your inner self—your old way of thinking, live changed lives] and become like children [trusting, humble, and forgiving], you will never enter the kingdom of heaven" (Matt. 18:3 AMP).

During a counseling session, an older man was reading a letter he wrote to and from the little boy inside. All of a sudden a locked door in his heart opened, and the little boy walked out. The man wept and wept, repeating over and over, "I found you. I found you. I found you." His tears were filled with pent-up pain and grief, but also with gratitude for the Father's opening that door. One thing he immediately noticed was the trust exuded by the boy. His inner child was ready, in a split second, to be vulnerable and spontaneous and trusting and to extend his little hand to grasp the hand of the grown-up man.

I believe that is exactly what Jesus was describing: revival that comes though the child. Revival that begins with the child in each of us.

PRAYER

Jesus, you did not only come to bring life to me today and tomorrow, but you also came to bring life abundantly to my past and to every broken piece within me. I realize that my spirit remembers every day of my life—from the moment you breathed me into my mother's womb. That is both awesome and frightening. Jesus, with your guidance, I want to welcome all of me home—every single part. I want to be converted and come like a child. Simple. Trusting. Spontaneous. Forgiving. Dependent. I want to experience revival that begins with my child within.

THOUGHTS AND REFLECTIONS

As we lay down our independence, we will find ourselves right in the Father's lap, a place of dependence we never need to leave again.

WHAT DOES GOD FEEL— ABOUT US?

I feel like I will be the lost lamb Jesus goes trudging into the cold dark to find—when all the rest of the good little flock are safely inside the barn—only to have him shake his head at me, pick me up with a sigh, and wonder why he puts up with me. I wonder if there was ever a point in my life where he looked at me with pleasure, or was he always disappointed with me? Was it something I did? Or just who I am?
—An Abuse Survivor

One of the themes we see in counseling is our clients' lack of awareness of and connection with how God feels—not about their sins or their failures or even their successes, but about them. About us. About *you*.

Many clients say they know how God sees them. After all, the Bible makes it plain, right? Yet when we ask, "How does the Father feel about you?" or "How did the Father feel when that happened to you?" they don't know what to say. They have never thought about how God *feels* when it comes to them personally. Once again we see the great disconnect between what our head knows and our heart feels.

PRAYER FOR THE JOURNEY

As we begin Week Four, pray with us for a personal revelation of the Father's heart in the journey ahead:

Father, there is much that I need to know about you and your heart. I need to see you for who you truly are and let that revelation go deep into my very core. I desire to feel and function more from my heart and less from my head. I invite you to open my heart and begin to remove anything that hinders me from feeling those things that are in your heart for me. Your Son, Jesus, lived from a passionate heart, and I want that as well. I believe you have made me in your image—feelings and all. Father, I want to feel what you feel, like Jesus, and be a reflection of that to others.

HOW LONG, O LORD, BEFORE YOU . . . ?

The God who has the whole world in his hands
has grace for the whole world in his heart.
—*Lewis Smedes*

I came up with a new idea for journaling: writing with invisible ink. Not really. But it is a good idea if you never want people to read your journals.

My journal writings started about thirty-five years ago and are stored in a box in my attic. I thought of writing a note on the box: "Do not read what is in this box. Please discard unopened box in the trash." However, knowing human curiosity, I think a request like that would probably guarantee that every journal got read in detail.

The reader would find interesting travel stories to Israel, Poland, Italy, and many islands and beaches. Many are God-stories with his fingerprints all over them. But most could probably be summed up in one phrase repeated several times in Scripture: "How long, O Lord?"

How long, O Lord, before you
    heal my loneliness?
    speak my name?
    heal my heart?
    heal my barrenness?

How long, O Lord, before you
>show me my destiny?
>heal my friend of cancer?
>save my family?

O Lord, look on me and answer me. Please.

How long, O Lord, before
>my darkness turns to light?
>I can enter into your rest?
>I can seek you and find you?
>my prayers no longer dribble off my chin onto the floor?
>love abounds, grace abounds, life abounds, breath abounds?

How long before you
>stop for me—
>pick me up—
>hold me—
>weep with me?

Sorry. Time out. Hit the pause button. Jerry just got out his guitar (which he hasn't done for months) and is looking through his music. He turns to me and says he is looking for the chords for "Psalm 13" and can't find them. "Well, that is a coincidence," I reply. "I was just journaling about Psalm 13."

But of course, it's *not* a coincidence. It's a God-incident, and it means to me that God still hears, still sees, and still knows *me*—even when I feel like the heavens are brass, like I am totally alone and am on my own.

PRAYER

Father, your truth always remains true, no matter what. Nothing can separate me from your love. You are always with me—always. You will never leave me or turn your back on me. There is nothing I could ever do to make you love me less. Father, I believe. Help my unbelief.

THOUGHTS AND REFLECTIONS

God is here. Right now. On your side. At your side. His arm is around you. He is actively seeking to help you and will never, ever leave you.

WAVES OF HIS AFFECTION

*Grace strikes us when we are in great pain and restlessness.
It strikes us when we walk through the dark valley of a
meaningless and empty life . . . when, year after year, the
longed-for perfection does not appear. . . . Sometimes at that
moment a wave of light breaks into our darkness,
and it is as though a voice were saying . . .
"You are accepted by that which is greater than you."
—Paul Tillich*

For the past seventeen years, St. George Island has been a yearly respite for Jerry and me. Although we sometimes use it as a place to get away and write, mainly we go there to decompress and rest. Lots of sleeping. Lots of good food. Lots of long walks on the beach. Lots of ball playing with our border collie, Grace. Many novels get read cover to cover. Many hours are spent staring at the waves, spellbound by their rhythm, mesmerized by their endless slap upon the shore. This year the waves in particular captured me.

If there ever was a time to just lie down and let God wash over me, now was that time. The year had been especially difficult, with many losses, especially the loss of my dad. Along with those losses were disappointments, hope deferred, loneliness, and a sense of abandonment by God. Quietly sitting on the beach staring at the waves was my way of surrendering once again and letting God's love wash over me.

However, it wasn't exactly his love that drew me in; it was his *affection*. I became mesmerized by the waves as they kept coming and coming and coming—one wave ending as a gentle touch on the beach, another several feet behind it rising up . . . and another . . . and another. And with every wave, I could hear the words of the Father: "There is no end to the affection I have for you." The waves of his affection still keep coming, keep forming, keep reaching out to me on the shore. All I can see on the horizon are more waves. Endless. Never stopping. Never ending. Unfathomable.

My Father is drawing me—inviting me—to embrace his affection for me, even on my worst day. Even when the heavens are brass, even when life makes no sense, even when I give up—even then, there is no end to the affection he has for me.

Upon leaving the island, I will still have unanswered questions. I will still have my wrestlings with God over life and love and hurt and darkness and death. But I am choosing to relax in his affection—affection that will never wane. Not now, not ever—an endless ocean of affection, a bottomless sea of his love.

Relax in his mystery. Just rest. Another wave is on its way . . . and look, there's another . . . and another . . .

Just relax and rest in him.

PRAYER

Read this prayer either out loud or whispered to yourself:

I am accepted. I am accepted. I am accepted by you who are greater than me. I will not try to do anything now. I will not seek for anything, or perform anything, or intend anything. I simply accept the fact that I am accepted by you, Father. And right now, experiencing that grace and resting in you is enough.

THOUGHTS AND REFLECTIONS

I can accept myself because God accepts me. I can love myself because God loves me. I know that I matter because God sent his Son, Jesus Christ, and through him he gave me the chance to live abundantly and eternally.

I LOVE THAT GOD FEELS

Can we imagine what it would be like to so move and excite
the heart of God that he would run to meet us, throw his arms
around us and kiss us, dress us in his best robe, and put rings
on our fingers? Can we imagine having the Creator of the
universe say to us, just as he said to Jesus Christ,
"You are my beloved son, and I like you?"
—Mike Mason

I am a big fan of God having emotions. I know he has emotions because you and I have them, and we are made in his image. In counseling, Jerry and I help people see how their parents' expressions of emotions during the growing-up years can impact their view of God as adults. For instance, if a parent was angry, controlling, and harsh when you were a child, or if one or both parents were gone a lot because of their work or ministry, or because of divorce, then you may have a more difficult time experiencing God as being close and interested in you, or understanding and affirming of you.

Using my own childhood as an example, if I projected the emotional makeup of my mother onto God today, I would see him as passive or distant. In a personal relationship with him, I would have difficulty *feeling* his closeness, interest, or compassion for me. He would probably not have time to spend with me and definitely would not pursue me. Like Mom, God would be there to run the household (the universe, in his case), which would mean no time for frivolous things like intimacy with me. Basically, I'd be on my own except when I needed to bother him. I would learn to just do my chores and my homework and not make waves.

If I projected my dad's emotional makeup onto Father God, I would see God as critical and perfectionistic. There would be no room for error, so to avoid a shaming comment or look, I would try to please him and be good. From my experience growing up, I would not necessarily see God as harsh and punishing but as one who sees and points out all my mistakes and flaws—maybe a little like Santa Claus who's "making a list, checking it twice, gonna find out who's naughty or nice." It reminds me of a chalkboard outside my family's kitchen that was used as a weekly tally of all the things I did wrong. I hated that chalkboard, and I snuck over and erased it whenever I had the chance.

Because children were to be seen and not heard in my household, the thought of running into the throne of grace into the lap of Abba Father was unconscionable to me. To approach God I would have to cover my head, keep my eyes down, knock gently, and tiptoe in—and probably genuflect once or twice. That is so different from how I would enter now—barging through the door, jumping up on his lap, and seeing the delight in his eyes. He has all the time in the world for me, just as if I were the only one.

This may seem a little strange, but one of my favorite emotions of the Father is his anger. Years ago, during a game of Bible Trivia in our small group, the question came up about God's nostrils. I never knew his nostrils made it into the Bible! For real—check it out for yourself in Psalm 18. God hears David's cry for help and thunders down from heaven. Riding a dark cloud with smoke coming out of his nostrils and accompanied by hailstones and lightning, he routes David's enemies. In my mind he is like a huge mama bear advancing toward a predator and roaring, "Don't you dare touch one of my cubs."

I remember the loneliness I felt as a teenager, sometimes sitting in my room crying, when no one ever came to check on me. Eventually I just came out of my room; no one even noticed I was gone. So the thought of the Father coming to be with me, protect me, and fight for me is very meaningful.

Like the prodigal father in Luke 15, God is not mad at me, furious with me, or condemning of me personally. My heavenly Father does not just bring me his list of all my failings and shortcomings, but he comes to encourage me in his love and not shame me "for my own good" or "to teach me a lesson."

Two Scripture passages deeply impact me as reflections of the emotions in the heart of the Father. Ponder the kind of Father they describe:

He tends his flock like a shepherd. He gathers the lambs in his arms and carries them close to his heart; he gently leads those that have young. . . . He gives strength to the weary and increases the power of the weak. Even youths grow tired and weary, and young men stumble and fall; but those who hope in the LORD will renew their strength. They will soar on wings like eagles; they will run and not grow weary, they will walk and not be faint (Isa. 40:11, 29–31).

"'This is what the Sovereign LORD says: I myself will search for my sheep and look after them. As a shepherd looks after his scattered flock when he is with them, so will I look after my sheep. I will rescue them from all the places where they were scattered on a day of clouds and darkness. I will bring them out from the nations and gather them from the countries, and I will bring them into their own land. I will pasture them on the mountains of Israel, in the ravines and in all the settlements in the land. I will tend them in a good pasture, and the mountain heights of Israel will be their grazing land. There they will lie down in good grazing land, and there they will feed in a rich pasture on the mountains of Israel. I myself will tend my sheep and have them lie down, declares the Sovereign LORD. I will search for the lost and bring back the strays. I will bind up the injured and strengthen the weak, but the sleek and the strong I will destroy. I will shepherd the flock with justice'" (Ezek. 34:11–16).

On my healing journey, I have experienced God's emotions—his very heart for me along the way. Not only does he allow me to share my messiness with him—my hurts, disappointments, struggles, fears, losses, and anger—but he also feels his own emotions right along with mine. I love that about God. What a gift to his children!

PRAYER

Father, it seems unfathomable that I, in my smallness, could move and excite your heart. That you would run to meet me, throw your arms around me. That you would kiss me on both cheeks and place your best robe on my shoulders and the most precious jeweled rings on my fingers.

(Can you picture this? Maybe you know that you are God's son or daughter, but can you believe that he actually *likes* you? That the Creator of the universe says to you, "You are my beloved child, and I like you"?)

Father, I so desperately need to know you more and experience your emotions toward me. Open up my heart and let me feel your heart. Remove any distortions I have about you and about myself that interfere with experiencing your truth. Thank you for hearing my prayer—my cry.

THOUGHTS AND REFLECTIONS

_____

_____

_____

_____

_____

_____

_____

_____

_____

_____

_____

_____

_____

_____

_____

_____

_____

_____

_____

_____

_____

_____

_____

_____

_____

_____

_____

_____

I felt God's feelings for me and my situation during the difficult stretch of my healing path—and that is what motivated me to keep going.

HE KNOWS OUR SMELL

*When my two-year-old son wanted his mom or dad to carry
him, he would hold out his hands saying, "Upple, Momma,
upple. Upple, Dadda, upple." In essence, "I'm tired. I'm afraid.
I'm weak. I'm too little. Pick me up. Carry me. Help me."
The spirit of brokenness helps us reach out our arms to the
Father saying, "Upple. Carry me. I am weak.
I am too little to do it on my own." I surrender.*
—Alan E. Nelson

Several years ago, a client gave us a painting of Jesus holding a little lamb
to his face. The picture demonstrated such tenderness, such closeness,
such warmth and love. We hung it in our counseling office where we also
held classes, small groups, and house church meetings. One night after
one of our gatherings, we noticed a young Jewish man standing in front
of the painting. He just stood there staring at it, mesmerized by it. After a
while we became curious and walked up next to him.

He told us what had so captured him. "You know that when Jesus called
God 'Father' when he taught his disciples to pray, it was shocking to place
God in such a close, human role. But Jesus went even further by calling God
'Abba'—the very intimate name of affection the children in the Hebrew cul-
ture would use toward a beloved father (similar to Daddy or Papa to us)."

He continued, "The English language does not do the name justice.
To us, Abba is not just the closeness of a daddy. To us it means he is so

close that he knows our smell. This picture captures the very essence of what it means for God to be our Abba. His very nose is in the crook of our neck, and he knows our smell."

It reminds me of my closeness to Jerry and how his aftershave smells. He has worn the same fragrance for as long as I can remember. Sometimes, as we sat up reading in bed, I would come across a sample card of a men's cologne and rub it across his wrist. We never did find one we liked. Afterward, the fragrance would often bother me so much that I had to get a wet washcloth and wipe it off his wrist. It was like I didn't know the person in bed next to me. It wasn't Jerry's smell!

So—going back to the painting of Jesus holding the lamb to his face: even today, remembering the story that young Jewish man shared, I am touched . . . and awed by that kind of Father. Many times I have brought that painting into the counseling room to share this story of how profound our Abba's love for each one of us is . . . how profound his closeness . . . his face tucked in our neck.

Abba. He knows our smell.

PRAYER

"Father." I often address you this way in my prayers to you. But many times I need to know that you are even more than my Father—as important as that is. I need to know that you know me and you have me, and you will never let me go. In those times I need to know you as my Abba. So today I choose to run to you and let you hold me close. And as I release all my fears and anxieties to you, I begin to rest in the truth that you really, really know me. You don't just know my name. You don't just know my voice. You don't just know what I look like. You know my smell. You are up close and very personal to me. Thank you for being that intimate. Thank you for being my Abba.

THOUGHTS AND REFLECTIONS

The Father's love for us is the same as the love he has for Jesus. To know this is very important. But to also feel this love from the Father takes it to another level, a level we believe God desires for all of us.

YOU ARE MY SUNSHINE

You are my sunshine, my only sunshine.
You make me happy when skies are gray
You'll never know, dear, how much I love you.
Please don't take my sunshine away.
—Jimmie Davis and Paul Mitchell

In our "previous lifetime," Jerry and I were university professors and administrators. After twenty years, we felt God drawing us to shift our lives and become Christian counselors in order "to heal the brokenhearted." Jerry also completed an additional degree to prepare him for a pastoral role, and a few years after establishing our counseling ministry, we began a house church. Our goal was to equip the saints so that each person knew they had a voice, knew their spiritual gifts, and knew they were revered by God as his precious child.

We once offered a class on hearing God's voice. A gifted and prophetic couple led the class, and about forty people attended. Each week included a break-away time to practice our new listening skills. I was in a small group with one of my former clients and her husband, who was a nominal believer at the time. We were directed to silently pray and ask God for something to share from him to the person on our right. I was struggling. I knew this woman next to me so well, knew so much of her history. How could I discern a word God wanted to share with her from what I already knew about her?

When it came my turn to share, I apologized for not hearing anything from God for her. I hesitated a moment and then quickly added under my breath, "Except that I kept hearing that old song, 'You are my sunshine, my only sunshine.'"

I thought the woman's husband was going to jump out of his chair. He looked at his wife and said, "Did you tell her about that song?" Now I was on the edge of my seat. I said, "I don't know what you mean. What does that song mean to you?"

Her husband told the group that when he and his wife were dating and she was feeling low and depressed, he would sing that song to her. It made her feel loved and lifted her spirits. He was beside himself (in a very good way) that God knew them and saw them, and that he would reveal private information no one else could possibly have known.

That night was a highlight in my life. I felt awed and humbled that God would share so precious a secret with me; mostly, though, I was in awe of the overwhelming love he expressed to that young man and his wife. He knew them. He saw them. He got up close and personal with them. He was a loving Father, they were his son and daughter, and that night he left his fingerprints on their hearts.

But here's a scary thought: What if I had not taken the risk and shared that song? It sounded pretty corny and off the wall to me. I felt embarrassed to share it, but thank God I stepped out and gave him a chance to wow us all. When Scripture refers to a "still, small voice," it means exactly that.

Thank you, Father, for not letting fear reign and rob your children of your presence and intimate love. Help us, Lord, to listen.

PRAYER

Father, you delight in me and enjoy me. You quiet me with your love, taking the time to simply be with me. You do not make it a point to remind me of all my mistakes and failures, of times when I didn't measure up. Instead, you draw me close to your heart like a little chick. You rejoice over me and sing songs to me, over me, and about me—songs as silly as "You Are My Sunshine." Thank you that I am that precious to you. Thank you for loving me "for keeps."

THOUGHTS AND REFLECTIONS

The Father says, "I know you, I see you, I am crazy about you, and I will heal every part of you."

GOING BACK TO GO FORWARD

What words describe the negative emotions I struggle with?
Alone. Bad. Guilty. Helpless. Hopeless. Inadequate.
Inferior. Insecure. Insignificant. Rejected. Self-condemning.
Stupid. Unaccepted. Unimportant. Worthless.
I know I shouldn't feel this about myself, but I can't
keep these emotions from overcoming me.
—A Pastor's Daughter

We are convinced that true, spiritual healing ultimately will result in our "coming home to the Father's house"—to his loving and healing heart. But in order for that to occur, we must be willing to journey back to our own house—that is, to the circumstances in which we grew up. Here is where the Lord often reveals how we were shaped by things that should not have happened to us but did, and by things that should have happened but did not.

It is on this journey home that he shows us aspects of our lives that align with his perfect plan and heals us from others that were not. On our pilgrimage, he allows us to find healing of our hearts in order to find him.

PRAYER FOR THE JOURNEY

As we begin Week Five, pray with us:

Lord Jesus, I desire to live fully alive, with the fruit of the Spirit—love, joy, and peace—active in my life. I know there are things that are affecting me and preventing me from living this way. I am willing to go back in order to go forward, and I invite you to show me anything that is necessary for me to see and deal with in order for healing to occur.

I cannot know these things unless you reveal them to me, and I know that you reveal what you plan to heal. Thank you for loving me enough to take me back to the home I grew up in so I can truly rest in the home you have prepared for me in your heart.

THAT'S A WOUND

If we conceal our wounds out of fear and shame,
our inner darkness can neither be illuminated
nor become a light for others.
—*Brennan Manning*

If you are asking Father God to heal you, you first have to know something is broken. So let us take you through a heart check.

When you have to be perfect to approve of yourself . . .

that's a wound.

When you can't let anyone know you are hurting . . .

that's a wound.

When you avoid anger at all cost . . .

that's a wound.

When you have been anxious for as long as you can remember . . .

that's a wound.

If you always have to

keep the peace

be right in order to be okay with yourself

be in control of your environment so you can rest . . .

that's a wound.

It's a wound if you

    can't say no.

    constantly compare yourself to others and fall short.

    are afraid to raise your hand even when you know the answer.

    stuff negative emotions or don't really feel much anyway.

    can't trust others because they may disappoint you or reject you.

If you

    lie when it would be easier to just tell the truth

    can't stand change

    are hypervigilant and can read a room as

        soon as you walk in

    have difficulty making decisions or finishing projects . . .

        any of those are wounds.

You've got a wound if you

    need people to like you.

    can't stand to have anyone mad at you.

    can't disappoint anyone.

    believe enmeshment is closeness.

    have difficulty asking for what you want or sharing your opinions

    worry about what others think of you.

If you are super responsible, so that everyone counts on you,

or you are super irresponsible, and nobody can trust your word . . .

    you have a wound.

If you don't take anyone or anything seriously . . .

If you won't tell anyone you are angry or hurt . . .

If you feel empty or alone even when you are with people . . .

    that's a wound.

Many times you may think, "That's just the way I am," but it points to something deeper. Something in your past—especially in your childhood and the family system you grew up in—created these wounds.

One of our clients recently said, "I thought I had a good childhood until Tuesday." (It was only the second day of a five-day intensive counseling session). When God opens the story of our past, he says, "It matters." It matters because it's true, whether we want to look at it or not. And when we partner with God to really see the child within each of us and own our story, Jesus will do what he set out to do from the beginning: heal the brokenhearted and set the captives free.

PRAYER

Father, you know me—every part of me. There are many things inside me that I have not understood. I haven't always known the "why" behind many of my thoughts, feelings, or actions. I haven't wanted to open up all the baggage from my past to put the pieces together. There are things in my life I have never told anyone—things better not remembered or addressed. At least, that is what I hoped when I buried them.

If I successfully stuffed those memories for this long, wouldn't it be best if I just kept it that way? I guess that's a no, right? And of course, you know everything and you still love me. Maybe with your help I could pull back the covers and find more of whom you made me to be. So I'm willing to do it—even though I'm scared. Thank you, Abba, that there is nothing in my past, present, or future that could make you love me less. Nothing. Nothing.

THOUGHTS AND REFLECTIONS

If we convince ourselves that what occurred to us didn't matter or was insignificant or unavoidable, then there isn't anything to invite God to heal.

MIRROR, MIRROR

Someday you will be old enough to read fairy tales again.
—C. S. Lewis

Do you remember the role of the mirror in the Walt Disney movie *Snow White and the Seven Dwarfs*? "Mirror, mirror on the wall, who is the fairest of them all?" Of course, the evil woman looking at her reflection is expecting the mirror to say, "You are the fairest of them all." She is so different from the clients we see. They never want to look at themselves.

Recently I started going through all our memorabilia stored in the attic. This was initiated by a weekend of cleaning out my parents' home after my mother died and my father was admitted to a dementia care facility. In one of the boxes, I found pictures from the "Snow Swirl" prom in twelfth grade, when Jerry and I were crowned king and queen. Alongside my somewhat-preserved flowers was my tiara. I threw away the flowers and placed the tiara on my lampshade.

Later that afternoon we were spending time with one of our favorite teens. At the close of our session, we walked her in front of the large mirror outside our office and asked her to say, "I love you, [her name]."

It was not an easy task. She told us over and over again that she could not do it. Just then I noticed the tiara, grabbed it, and placed it on her head. With tears streaming down her face, she whispered to the girl in the mirror, "I love you."

When she pressed through and said, "I love you," the enemy, who is a liar and a deceiver, lost some of his grip. A couple of months later, the God "who never speaks to her personally" spoke to her personally, out of the blue, and told her how lovable and acceptable she is to him. She could hardly believe it because the words were too good to be true. But they were amazingly true and amazingly God.

Another male client wrote this about the mirror exercise: "Today I make a practice of looking at myself in the mirror and encouraging myself. Instead of trying to do right and be something, I am trusting and seeking the Lord. I am wrapping my arms around the truth that, like Jesus, I am my Father's son, in whom he is well pleased."

The words "I love you" continue to be a powerful prayer in the lives of our clients. Jerry and I have walked many over to the mirror, had them look themselves straight in the eyes, and then encouraged them to verbalize a love for themselves that agrees with God's own deep love for them. This prayer of declaring our love for ourselves is one of the hardest and most powerful prayers we can pray to break lies and strongholds and to free our hearts to love.

How to Do the Mirror Exercise

You can do the Mirror Exercise at home—right now, if you wish.

Using a mirror of any size—it could be a full-length floor mirror or the one on your medicine cabinet—look directly and deeply into your own eyes and speak the following affirmations. They are truths that agree with how God our Father feels toward you, truths that make him smile. Speaking them will feel awkward at first, but repeat this exercise daily until you believe it. Remember, every time you do so aloud, you take a whack at the lies and the liar.

I love you, (<u>your name</u>). I am fearfully and wonderfully made.

Lord, I am a precious treasure to you. I am the one you love dearly. I am the apple of your eye, and you celebrate the day I was born. Father, I was on your mind from the beginning of time. You call me by name and say, "You are mine." There is nothing I could ever do to make you love me more. There is nothing I could ever do to make you love me less. Lord, you call me special—a daughter/son of the King. I am your treasure and delight. You love me, God, and I choose to love myself.

Mirror, mirror on the wall, I am the one the Father calls—
Calls my name, saying, "You are mine.
I have loved you from the beginning of time.
Mirror, mirror on the wall,
YOU, precious one, are the loveliest of all."

PRAYER

Lord, I believe. Help my unbelief.

THOUGHTS AND REFLECTIONS

So I accept the fact that I am important, that I have value and worth. I have eternal value. I love myself and I like myself, every part, because I choose to love who God loves—and that is me.

GREETING CARDS

God makes us totally dependent on parents or caregivers for
the first five years of our lives. Our parents become like gods
to us. In a perfect world, this would be a good thing.
—The Missing Commandment: Love Yourself

I (Denise) had a brilliant idea one day to keep a greeting card rack right outside our counseling office. The display would only have cards for mothers and fathers, whether for birthdays, anniversaries, or the holidays. One of the assignments we would give each client would be to pick out a card for their mom and their dad and bring it into the counseling office to share during their session.

If you were picking out a card, what would it say?

"I've always looked up to you."

"You were always there for me—you guided me and supported me."

"Thanks for showing me what a great marriage looks like."

"I am the person I am today because of you." (Either that's a good thing or you have some unresolved issues to address).

"You taught me more than you'll ever know." (This could be a tricky one too).

Or maybe you would lean toward a more generic message: "Have a nice day." "Bless you." "Thinking of you today."

You might find it easier to send a more humorous card that doesn't require a heartfelt connection: Garfield with a birthday cake pop-up. An another-year-older joke. A childhood memory, like "I forgive you, Mom, for cutting my bangs too short. Happy Mother's day anyway!" (That is one my sister actually sent to my mom.)

If you wonder what needs did or did not get met by your mother or father when you were growing up, read some greeting cards. Look at which cards you could never send. Maybe even pause and let yourself feel the loss, the sadness, the anger, or the indifference from not having the warm experiences and feelings conveyed in some of the cards.

When Jerry and I go card shopping, we often find cards we wish were true for us. One Father's Day card read, "The Imprint of a Father Remains Forever on the Life of a Child." Wow! Stop for a moment. Ponder that statement. What a precious truth for some sons and daughters—yet for others, it's their worst nightmare. Unfortunately, in counseling, we see way too much of the latter.

Next time you are in the grocery store, stop at the card rack, and instead of looking for a card for someone else, look at the cards you would like others to buy for you. With the Father's help, maybe you can make card shopping a nice experience for the special people in your life.

PRAYER

Father, thank you that you are the perfect Father with a perfect mother-heart. Your strength on one side and your tenderness on the other do not conflict. Some days, I need you to war on my behalf. On others, I need you to hide me in the cleft of a rock, safe from my enemies. There are times when I need you to run to me and embrace me in my fallenness—to collect my tears in a bottle and add some of your own, just as you cried over Jerusalem. There are other times when I need you to continue to work on the mansion you are building for yourself in my heart. To sing over me with a song only you and I know. To draw me into your rest in a way I have never known.

How can you be and do all these things for me as though I am the only one? How wonderful and awesome you are! Father God, I am asking you to leave the imprint of a Father that remains forever on the life of this child—me.

THOUGHTS AND REFLECTIONS

The biggest influence on how a person sees God is not their knowledge of the Scriptures. It is the representation or misrepresentation of God, which that person saw mirrored by their parents.

I THOUGHT I HAD A GOOD CHILDHOOD

Today the heart of God is an open wound of love. . . .
He longs for our presence. And he is inviting you—
and me—to come home, to come home to where we belong,
to come home to that for which we were created.
His arms are stretched out wide to receive us.
His heart is enlarged to take us in.
—Richard Foster

We can't tell you how many clients come to counseling believing they had a good childhood. After all, our parents are like gods to us as little children. There is also a sense of loyalty that often arises as a protection of them:

"Sure it was rough at times, but we never went hungry."

"My dad was a hard worker, and he never missed one of my games."

"My mom sometimes drank too much, but she's not an alcoholic."

"Mom was controlling and demanding, but she helped me build great organizational skills."

"My parents were always fighting when I was growing up, but they have mellowed a lot since and are great with the grandkids now."

We often reply, "Wow, that's a pretty soft landing you gave them. You seem to rush into minimizing, rationalizing, and putting a spin on your parents' behavior to take them off the hook. So what do you ever need to forgive them for? Have you spent any time at all grieving what you lost when these things happened to you? Did it even matter? Did it matter to God? Did he have a different plan for the way you were parented? Does God hold your parents responsible, or does he just give them a pass for when your father was abusive and your mother didn't protect you? A pass for when you laid in bed at night trying to muffle their fighting?

"If your parents deserve such loyalty, let's imagine your own son or daughter growing up in your place. Same parents, same conditions. You only get to watch, like a fly on the wall. You can't rescue your child until they are eighteen."

Reality hits. Typical reactions are, "That will never happen." "Over my dead body." Or, tearfully, "No, that would not work for me. I would want to get my child out of there."

That's where the healing starts: with that gut-level honesty. Now God can begin restoring hearts that come to him with their pain, shame, loss, and fears.

There is one person to whom loyalty does belong, and that is our spouse: "I've got your back. You can trust me to be there. We're a team."

Sometimes one or both parents of a spouse feel threatened by such loyalty. When a husband or wife has to check in with a parent daily; when one spouse has to spend every Friday night at his or her mother's house; when every vacation has to be spent with parents; when there is a push-pull between both sets of parents for control . . . that is loyalty misplaced.

After God, our first loyalty is to our spouse and children. We are asked to leave and cleave, and when we don't, or when we delay the split, it causes unbelievable stress in the marriage relationship.

Couples in counseling can be brutally honest about each other, yet are often very protective when talking about their parents. One client's abusive father was convicted for selling child pornography of her and many other children. Yet she still gave him high scores on parenting!

In our counseling, we never set out to throw parents under the bus or "blame" them. However, clients need to deal with the truth of what really happened to them in their childhood—not from their perspective but from God's. We always add to our prayer, "Father, reveal no more than is necessary to heal the child inside." That means we can put our trust in him to lead the process

Trust Abba. He has your back.

PRAYER

Father, I love you. Thank you for loving me, your child. Thank you for asking me for a return favor: for me to love myself like you do. That's a little harder and somewhat awkward. But I realize now that loving myself is a pivotal link to loving you and loving others.

I am sorry I have not always seen myself as lovable. Growing up, I was sensitive to criticism, yet my worst critic has always been myself. I could come to you confessing all my faults, failures, and sins, and you would respond by throwing me a party. How great, how wide, how deep is your love for me. I love you, Papa, and I want to love myself the way you love me. I choose to love myself. I know you don't make junk.

THOUGHTS AND REFLECTIONS

We must be willing to journey back to our own house—that is, to the circumstances in which we grew up. We must see it this time through God's eyes.

HEALING A DISCONNECTED HEART

Deep down inside a child's inner world are a multitude of needs, questions, hurts, and longings. . . .
The busy, insensitive, preoccupied parent, steamrolling through the day, misses many a cue and sails right past choice moments, never to be repeated again.
—Paul Tournier

An *attachment disorder* is the inability to form loving and lasting relationships, to give or receive love or affection, or to trust others. Does any of that sound like you or someone you love?

Jerry and I both identified with unhealthy bonding issues in our early childhood. In God's plan, we are to connect with our mothers at birth (and even in the womb). This establishes trust as a foundation for our entire lives. If we form healthy and consistent bonds early on, healthy attachments most often will continue in our relationships as adults. Unfortunately, when a child misses that window of opportunity to bond with an adult, an attachment disorder is likely to result. Most often this occurs within the first three years of life.

Jerry and I both experienced a breach in healthy attachment from the very beginning of our lives. We were both the opposite sex our parents wanted. Jerry was unplanned and came at a bad time financially. I was told that my mother was depressed after I was born and that I cried all the time. Not much parental connection and belonging for either of us.

Maybe as a little child you were abandoned through divorce, addictions, illness, or neglect. Maybe you experienced trauma from accidents, the death of a parent, foster care, adoption, or emotional, physical, or sexual abuse. Or perhaps, like many others, you have a disconnected or detached heart simply because your parents were emotionally unavailable or distant.

One woman told us her traumatic birth story. After two stillbirths, her mother was warned never to get pregnant again. But she did, and the doctor told her not to expect that the baby would live. So the parents did nothing to prepare for bringing a baby home. They didn't even think of a name. Few people even knew the mother was pregnant.

As soon as the baby was born, she was taken to intensive care. She stayed there for three days, with no family visiting her or holding her. The doctor didn't want the mother to bond with a baby that was doomed to die. But she didn't die. Two shell-shocked parents finally took their baby girl home. But her mother never allowed herself to bond with her baby, because it would hurt too much if she lost her.

Another woman was estranged from her teenage daughter. The child, born with a heart defect, had been poked and prodded by specialists early in life and required emergency open-heart surgery when she was only two. After coming out of the anesthesia, instead of reaching out for her mommy, the toddler turned her head away. A dramatic disconnect occurred that day, and the child remained indifferent to her mother's presence ever since.

People with attachment issues desire love and acceptance, yet strangely, they reject it when it is offered them. This happens because the trauma, loss, and rejection they experienced as children actually changed their brain.

A person who spends the first few years of his or her life in a physically or emotionally painful environment organizes his or her brain to create an unhealthy style of survival behavior. One of the most common behaviors is to avoid pain at all cost. Therefore, a person with attachment issues learns to resort to denial rather than rational thought. When the emotions of fear or sadness are triggered, a child's brain denies those feelings. It's how the brain protects the child from emotional pain.

Attachment problems vary in severity. As adults, we may be able to quickly identify some of the following common symptoms in our lives and our relationships. As you go through the list, ask the Father to show you where you still struggle. Those will be areas to invite him to heal.

Symptoms of Attachment Problems

Which of the following describe you?

- Avoid conflict.
- Deny that you are wrong.
- Have to be in control.
- Have difficulty showing or feeling compassion.
- Don't easily trust.
- Can't easily give or receive affection or love.
- Resist care or help from others.
- Need sex to reduce anxiety or feel accepted.
- Are easily provoked and defensive.
- Lie to or manipulate others.
- Are argumentative or hostile.
- Lack self-control.
- Struggle with addictive behavior.
- Don't do anger.
- Are hypervigilant (you can read a room).
- Feel isolated and depressed.
- Have to have the answer.
- Are superficially nice.
- Feel blamed by others.
- Feel alone, even around others.

That's quite a list, isn't it? Now here is a fascinating insight on how God wired our brain. As very young children we store our emotions in our midbrain; storage for rational thought hasn't developed yet in the front of the brain. So later in life, if we go to counseling that is more reasoning or cognitive in nature, the midbrain is not accessed and our stored emotions from early childhood are not dealt with.

This scientific information validates why we have to let the Father take us on a journey back to our home of origin, where the damage occurred and the pain was suppressed. It also explains why the grief process is so critical. We must "feel it to heal it" and "grieve it to leave it."

That is why, in our counseling ministry, we go for the underlying issues. We see so many breakthroughs because we tap into the part of the brain where the child denied his or her emotions as a form of defense and survival.

The great news is that we have a Father in heaven who can go back into the past and heal us there so we can be dramatically transformed in the present. We were never made merely to survive. We were made to live and thrive!

PRAYER

Father, my eyes are being opened to the ways my heart became disconnected so long ago. I did not realize the negative things that happened to me early in my childhood really mattered. I thought that what was past, was past. Yet I see now that some of my behaviors as an adult point to a younger, fragmented part of my development.

Father, I know I wasn't a mistake. I wasn't the problem. It wasn't my fault. Please take my hand and walk with me back through my childhood. I'm willing to look wherever you show me—in the basement, in my bedroom, at the dinner table. You know where the memories are stored. I'm willing to go through the pain so you can heal my heart—so I can love you more, love myself, and then love others.

THOUGHTS AND REFLECTIONS

_____
_____
_____
_____
_____
_____
_____
_____
_____
_____
_____
_____
_____
_____
_____
_____
_____
_____
_____
_____
_____
_____
_____
_____
_____
_____
_____
_____

The Father showed me that I mattered, and therefore what had happened to me as a child also mattered. And because it mattered to him, it should also matter to me.

FOUNDATIONAL BUILDING BLOCKS: TRUST AND IDENTITY

A part of you was left behind very early in your life:
the part that never felt completely received.
You want yourself to be one.
So you have to bring home the part of you that was
left behind. When you befriend your true self and
discover that it is good and beautiful, you will see Jesus there.
Where you are most human, most yourself, weakest,
there Jesus lives.
Bringing your fearful self home is bringing Jesus home.
—Henri Nouwen

The first and most foundational building block in life is trust. Trust is formed in the first nine months after birth. All the other building blocks—independence, identity, confidence, and initiative—are built on trust.

Basic trust lies at the core of self-confidence and freedom from what others think. Trusting in who we are as a valued human being safeguards us from being easily manipulated and controlled by others, so we don't lose track of who we are or become a non-person. A strong foundation of trust provides us with the freedom to entrust our heart to others and to God.

The second major developmental stage in children is identity, which occurs between the ages of two and four. At this stage, we make one of the most impactful decisions in our entire life: either "I am me and I'm okay" or "I am me and I am *not* okay.

If "I am me and I am okay," then I have the freedom to be different from you. I have the courage to say no. I can be separated from others and still feel safe. On the other hand, if "I am me and I am *not* okay," then I will learn to project a false self and pretend to be who I think you want me to be. I cannot say no because I do not want to offend you or risk your rejection. I am certain that if you saw the real me, you wouldn't like me—because at my core, I don't like me either.

Thankfully, God came to heal the brokenhearted and set the captives free. And when God heals our broken heart, our life is transformed from the inside out.

PRAYER FOR THE JOURNEY

As we begin Week Six, pray with us for the Father's loving guidance in the journey ahead:

Father, I want to live from a place of trust—trusting in you and your goodness and trusting others who you say are trustworthy. I also want to be able to trust my own heart, which you have renewed by my faith in you.

Lord, help me to see if trust was broken in my early development. If so, I invite you to bring healing to that broken part of me. Father, if my identity as your child has been impaired from this early wounding, heal and restore me and help me to rest in whom you've made me to be. I ask that you would help me to love the little child inside me the way you do. I need you, and I need every part of me that you created. Only you can bring about this healing and restoration in me. I choose to trust you with myself.

WHEN THE BAGS ARE EMPTY

Hurt moves the heart toward healing. Therefore, even if you're living in hurt, you are better off in the hurt than to not have it at all—to not feel is to not be alive, although sometimes being fully alive is excruciating.
—*Chip Dodd*

When we talk to someone about our "baggage," we are usually referring to negative issues, failures, or trials from our past that are still affecting us in some way. These problems may stem from our childhood, our previous relationships, jobs, friends, or family. Whenever it happened, we realize there is still something back there that is somehow negatively impacting us currently. We may talk to a counselor or join a support group to help us "unpack our baggage." We learn to process in greater detail those issues from the past that continue to work against us—and to ultimately find healing for these issues.

When most people think about dealing with their baggage, they generally think about events or memories from their earlier years that have been hurtful and have left an imprint on them. This, for example, could include times when a child was subjected to emotional, physical, or sexual abuse by a parent or family member.

But what if you don't have any significant memories of being wounded as a child, yet you know you aren't living from a place of emotional wholeness? This has been one of the most important yet frequently overlooked questions for many of the people we have counseled over the years.

People come to us struggling with anger, depression, anxiety, loss of purpose and calling, relational conflict, addictions, or grief. They may also be having difficulty in connecting with God on an intimate level. Yet when they reflect on their early developmental years—the period when identity is shaped—they cannot identify any specific negative memories. There is nothing they can remember that could have caused early wounding and the subsequent struggles they are now experiencing. In fact, some individuals have very few memories at all for the first six or seven years of life. When they enter into a process of "unpacking their baggage" from childhood, their bags appear to be empty.

But they are not.

Without minimizing the impact of traumatic childhood events, we want to focus here on a different type of wounding: the wounding from "acts of omission" versus "acts of commission." When a child's needs are not met—needs God designed to be met by the primary caregivers—there will be significant consequences in later years.

Wounds of omission can be just as damaging as overt wounding. Sometimes they are even more damaging because they are so well hidden and difficult for the person to identify. The fact that the person is struggling emotionally but has no specific memories to validate such struggles can result in a great deal of shame and self-condemnation: "What's wrong with me? Why can't I have it all together like everyone else? Maybe I just need to try harder." The person may conclude, "I'll never measure up. I'm the problem."

During a counseling process many years ago, I (Jerry) began to realize that there were empty places in my heart that did not receive all that I needed when I was young. Although I also had more overt wounds, I soon realized that some of my deeper wounding came from areas of lack.

There were things I needed that I just didn't get. And believe me, our empty places will still cry out to be filled in our adulthood. Unfortunately, for most of us, they do so in unhealthy ways.

One morning over coffee, Denise turned to me and asked me to close my eyes and ask God what he wanted to show me. As I did, the Lord showed me something I didn't expect. I saw the inside of a room that was very empty. I knew this room represented my heart. God continued to show me other rooms that were just as empty or barren. This brought tears to my eyes, and I could feel his pain and grief in seeing my heart this way. Instead of a heart filled with signs of life, my heart could not really feel, just function. I looked like I had it together on the outside, but my heart-house was sterile.

(Truthfully, doesn't it sometimes seem like *not* feeling could be a good thing, especially if we want to stay focused, keep negative thoughts at bay, and keep our facade up? Trust me, it's a dead end.)

Opening up my heart to God and inviting him into my empty places, I began to grieve what it cost me to not have significant needs met in my childhood. I *knew* I was loved by my parents, but did I *feel* loved (emphasis on feeling versus knowing)? Did I *feel* loved, special, precious, prized, valued, and significant? Did I feel deserving of the very best? Did I feel celebrated for who I was—that I had a special place in the family? Did I feel cared for and affirmed through appropriate touch? If the response is no to any of these questions, a "love deficit" is created in a little child's heart. Consequently the child will often feel alone, insignificant, inadequate, and unworthy.

I began to feel the Father's grief for me over the empty heart-rooms that he desired to be fully furnished. It took a little longer for me to recognize the areas of wounding where I just didn't get enough of my needs met to be truly whole. I learned that even when the bags are empty, there is still a healing work the Father desires to do.

PRAYER

Dear Father God,

Please open my heart to see places in me that did not receive what was needed and where I am still being affected today. I am willing to feel what you feel about these empty places in me, so that I can ultimately be healed.

Father, it is so healing and life giving to my soul and spirit to know that before I could even do one thing, quote one Scripture, or sing one worship song, you first loved me. And not just that—you first cherished me. You first desired me. You first celebrated me . . . and chose me . . . and pursued me. Thank you for ascribing such unfathomable worth to me.

Love,

Your Child (who loves you back)

THOUGHTS AND REFLECTIONS

Some of the most severe emotional impact on a child and future adult is not just from abusive actions, but from the absence of loving actions.

YOU ARE A LETTER

Your very lives are a letter that anyone can read by just looking at you. Christ himself wrote it—not with ink, but with God's living Spirit; not chiseled into stone, but carved into human lives—and we publish it.
—Paul the Apostle (2 Corinthians 3:3 MSG)

You are a letter. Your life—all of it (the good, the bad, and the ugly)—is a letter. You become a published letter by allowing the Holy Spirit to write your story on your heart. From a yielded and vulnerable place, clients have written letters to the wounded parts of themselves that have never been exposed to the love of Christ. Listen to the words of these letters with the ears of your heart. Imagine yourself in some of them, and consider whether you believe these stories—and your own story—matter to God.

Letter to the Child Inside Me

I am writing to the child inside me who was physically hurt, emotionally abused, and shamed again and again. You cried until there were no tears left, only anger. I want you to know God wept over you and cared that you hurt. It's time now that we release all the vows you made to protect yourself. You had no one you could trust, so you steeled your heart, even with God.

I want to hold your hand—one hand in yours and my other hand in the Father's. I want you to meet God and allow him to take away all the shame, all the fear, and all the anger. You were a child, and you were NOT responsible. Did you hear me? It wasn't your fault.

Letter from God to a Grown Man

After one client wrote a letter to his inner child, he waited prayerfully and wrote what he felt was coming from the Father. Here is what he sensed.

My son, I see all your pain and frustration. I have always been right beside you, even when you didn't feel me there. You were emotionally abandoned and orphaned at an early age. You trusted no one but yourself and did everything for yourself. I am here now to open up your wounded heart and teach you to trust me.

My command to you every day is for you to love yourself more today than you did yesterday. You need to be kind to yourself and love yourself, forgive yourself—even for your ugliest thoughts that cause you shame. You feared that one simple, bad thing would separate you from my love. Reach out to that little boy inside you who is still afraid of making just one mistake that will cause him to be rejected—again. I am asking you to love that scared little boy for me. When you do, you will be living from my heart.

Letter to Little Girl

Dear little one, please forgive me for rejecting and hating you for so many years. I have believed the lies sown in your heart: You are worthless. You can't do anything right. You deserved the abuse.

That is not who you are. You are a very special little girl, and I am so sorry for never seeing you that way. I'm so sorry that you had to shut down emotionally, just to stop the pain. You don't have to do that anymore, because I am here to listen to your broken heart. We can both go to Daddy God, and He will hold us, protect us, and show us who we really are.

You are safe. You can trust me again. I will never shame you as I did before. For the first time, maybe you can let go of all the fear and shame. Daddy God loves you, and so do I.

Letter to Little Boy

Hello little boy, I am writing this letter to connect with you. Today I am beginning to understand how much you were hurt and left alone. What pain did you go through? Even from the womb you were not wanted. You were lonely growing up and never seemed to be able to perform good enough. People said, "Your parents gave you everything you needed." Well, they gave you what you needed for your physical body, but they abandoned you emotionally and didn't guide your spirit. I wish I could have whispered in your ear, "You are special. I am proud of you."

I am truly sorry for locking you up, for hiding you, for ignoring you, for pretending you do not even exist anymore. I avoided feeling your hurt and pain. I avoided shame at all cost and I am sorry. Please forgive me.

Prayer to God

Father God, father me. Father God, father us.

PRAYER

Father, I know that you love me and actually delight in me . . . every part of me. I want you to show me how I have negatively seen myself and criticized myself. I want nothing to block my heart from deeply experiencing your love for me, so I can then give it away. I'm willing to begin that process right now. Here I go:

Dear little me . . .

THOUGHTS AND REFLECTIONS

God is asking you to stop and bring those parts of your heart back to him and allow his to heal you and establish you on the right path—his path.

REPAIR MY HEART

God will heal and mend.
It's what he does;
it's who he is.
—Kaitlyn Bouchillon

Shortly after giving my heart to Jesus many years ago, I (Jerry) had a profound experience I have never forgotten. Denise and I were living in Houston at the time, and one morning, while I was in the shower, I actually "heard" these words: *A repairer of the breach, a restorer of paths to dwell in.* Whether what I heard was audible to my ears or only to my heart, I do not know. But I do know that it was loud and clear. It was a surreal experience.

The words sounded like they might have come from the Bible, but I had never heard or read them before, and I had no idea where to look. I finally found them in Isaiah 58:12: "And your people will rebuild the ancient ruins; You will raise up *and* restore the age-old foundations [of buildings that have been laid waste]; You will be called Repairer of the Breach, Restorer of Streets with Dwellings" (AMP).

My first question was, "God, this must be from you, but why are you sharing it with me?" I read further and found that Isaiah was prophesying to the Jewish people who would one day return from exile in Babylon. He was describing the physical rebuilding and restoring of the walls and the temple in Jerusalem that God's people would undertake.

But what message was I supposed to take away from this experience?

Although I had never considered a calling to counseling or ministry, I believe the Lord was placing that desire in my heart and wanting me to know it was important to him. His words are just as meaningful to me today as when I first heard them.

So what *was* God saying? I believe he was telling me that our hearts are in need of repair and need to be restored, and he was calling me to bring his healing and restoration to others. What I didn't realize at the time was that he was first going to repair and restore *my* heart before he released me to help others. But in the next few years, I discovered how greatly I myself needed healing. As I pursued it with a Christian counselor, God opened my eyes to the great need for healing in Christ's body, the church.

You see, all of us have broken places within. All of us grew up in homes with varying degrees of dysfunction. We have breaches in our hearts, holes, wounds we received from caregivers. Wounds from things that should not have occurred when we were children, and wounds from the lack of things we needed. Some of these broken places have been lying waste for many years and have passed on from generation to generation within families.

Walking into churches on Sunday, I could "see" the hurt and pain in so many of God's people—hurt and pain hidden behind masks. By working on my heart and allowing me to see the hearts of others through his eyes, God drew me into a very different calling than I had ever imagined.

Back to the words I heard in the shower. Those words are timeless. They were spoken thousands of years ago, but the Father was speaking them that day to *me*—and he is still speaking them today to as many as will listen. He longs to repair our broken areas and restore places for us to flourish—in our homes, our relationships, our vocations, our interests, and all aspects of life. As the world becomes increasingly uncertain and unstable, God wants our "foundation" to be raised up and secured so that in the days ahead we can stand.

How does a person begin? Invite the Father to show you your heart and reveal where you are broken and need healing. When necessary, seek help from others, such as a counselor, to help you on our journey. As you submit to the healing of your heart, you can live more fully from a secure place in him. And don't be surprised if you hear him speaking to your heart at the least expected time and in the most unexpected ways. Who knows? You might end up becoming a repairer and restorer of others.

PRAYER

Father, help me see what I need to see at this time—the condition of my own heart and soul—and invite you into those places in me that still need your touch. Your love. I give you permission to repair and rebuild the places in me that are still in a state of disrepair. I welcome your work of restoration so that I can receive more of your love and then love you more, love myself more, and give love to others freely. Thank you for being the "repairer of the breach and a restorer of paths to dwell in." Thank you for making me your apprentice.

THOUGHTS AND REFLECTIONS

_____

_____

_____

_____

_____

_____

_____

_____

_____

_____

_____

_____

_____

_____

_____

_____

_____

_____

_____

_____

_____

_____

_____

_____

_____

_____

_____

_____

_____

_____

If true healing is to occur, the love of the Father has to get to the places—often very young places—where the injury occurred.

IS THERE A DOOR NUMBER THREE?

Our todays are shaped by our yesterdays.
What is past may also be a prison—a prison of recurring
painful patterns of thinking, feeling and relating.
—Sandra Wilson

When I (Jerry) was a kid, I used to watch *Let's Make a Deal*, hosted by Monty Hall. For those of you who remember the show (and those of you who still watch it), the contestant must choose which one of three doors he wants opened. Behind one is a major prize, while behind the other two are booby prizes. Sometimes the host of the show will open one of the three doors, revealing that it is not the one holding the grand prize. Then the contestant must choose between one of the two remaining.

Often we ask our clients, "Is there a door number three?" Why? Because the choices they communicate to their spouse, children, or others are rigid and end up controlling those they are closest to. You probably know someone like this. Or maybe you live with someone like this. Or . . . you *are* someone like this.

What we're really talking about is someone who operates with black-and-white thinking. There is no room for gray. Another way such thinking shows up is when a person judges everything as either right or wrong. Again, no discussion allowed. This person is the opposite of the one who rarely voices an opinion or preference. You've probably encountered that kind as well.

Interestingly, both types—those with rigid boundaries and strong opinions and those with very loose boundaries and few opinions—can come from similar dysfunctional homes of origin and childhood wounding. But let's focus on the first type—the one with rigid boundaries, or what we would call "walls."

Why would we end up counseling someone with this personality? It doesn't sound like such a person would ever feel the need to seek help. After all, they've pretty much figured out the problem, and the answer is to "just do this" or "stop doing that," whatever this or that happens to be. Usually, though, this style of relating eventually results in a damaged relationship—like a marriage—and the threat of a spouse's leaving creates a crisis that can no longer be ignored.

We are describing a strong case of rigidity here, and of right-versus-wrong thinking—someone you probably wouldn't enjoy spending much time with. But this controlling, black-and-white thinking doesn't have to manifest in an undesirable personality. Some of these people exhibit very desirable traits; nevertheless, certain areas in their lives display significant controlling behaviors which are particularly evident to those closest to them—the ones who feel controlled.

Where does such conduct come from?

Original research on the effects of growing up in an alcoholic home revealed a host of negative effects that manifested in adulthood. They include the rigid, black-and-white, right-versus-wrong thinking and the relational styles we've just described. But why?

Many alcoholic home environments—particularly those where the alcoholic parent becomes more aggressive when drinking—create a fearful, out-of-control atmosphere. A child exposed to it has no power to stop or change it. Often the child—and later the adult—begins to bring order to the things he or she *can* control. Maybe it's only the condition of their bedroom, but at least the child can bring order to that.

It has long been recognized that this dynamic isn't limited to alcoholic households. Children growing up in any significantly dysfunctional home respond in a similar way, and they bring their behavior and its underlying issues with them into adulthood. People who need to have things in control, and who find it difficult to release control to others or do things differently than they have in the past, are dealing with fear at their core. It's not the type of fear we typically relate to, such as a fear of heights or snakes or the like; it's deeper and more foundational. Anxiety rooted in early childhood is what drives controlling behaviors. And that core fear often operates in tandem with toxic shame (the kind that says you're fundamentally not okay) and pride ("I can do it; I don't need anyone or anything").

If you're married to or work with someone who exhibits controlling behaviors, you end up either butting heads with that person or else just acquiescing and ultimately getting "lost" in the relationship—especially if you are the spouse in a marriage.

"Wait a minute," you might be thinking, "isn't it good to know right from wrong and to stand on the truth? Didn't Jesus communicate truth and even say, 'You will know the truth, and the truth will set you free'?" (John 8:32).

Yes, truth is very important. However, Jesus came "full of grace *and* truth." (John 1:14, emphasis added). Jesus didn't operate with black-and-white thinking. That is why he often drove the religious leaders nuts. Jesus applied truth to every situation he faced and didn't operate from a default mechanism—black versus white, right versus wrong—that was rooted in woundedness. Think about the woman caught in adultery or the man with the shriveled hand whom Jesus healed on the Sabbath (John 8:1–11; Mark 3:1–5). Jesus was able to discern when and when not to act, when to speak or not speak. And he never compromised truth or the heart of his Father in any situation.

Ask yourself these questions:

- Do I frequently find it hard to yield to another opinion or way of doing something?
- Do I feel I need to be perfect in certain areas, and do I have little grace for myself when I fail or make a mistake? (Perfectionism is another result of core wounding.)

- Do my choices often focus on what I feel is needed or right, and do they often trump the choices of others around me?
- Do I find that emotional intimacy and connectedness in my closest relationships take a back seat to my subtle or not-so-subtle need to be in control of my environment?
- Do I find it hard to feel the full range of emotions—unable to feel God's feelings for myself and for others?

If your answer to any of these questions is yes, stop and ask God to help you see why. He will be delighted to open up that door with you. He knows how the wound that lies behind it is hurting your heart and hindering your ability to love fully—first him, then yourself, and then others. After all, it is God's love that pushes out fear and anxiety (1 John 4:18), and he came to heal our broken hearts and set us free.

So if you're asked sometime, "Is there a door number three?" check yourself and see how inflexible or rigid you are. There might be a younger part of you that is in control and is crying out to be healed.

PRAYER

Father, I want to be able to fully rest and to trust you more. I know you are trustworthy and that you have also placed people in my life whom I can trust. What holds me back? Why do I find myself at times "majoring on the minors?" Why do I struggle with yielding as much as I do? Open up my heart and help me see if I am operating from a wounded place that started a long time ago. Help me to trust you with that which is so important to you—my heart. I want to live from a place of truth and grace like you did, Jesus, and not have to compromise in any way. Lead me in the way I need to go. Be my shepherd in this and all areas of my life.

THOUGHTS AND REFLECTIONS

_____

_____

_____

_____

_____

_____

_____

_____

_____

_____

_____

_____

_____

_____

_____

_____

_____

_____

_____

_____

_____

_____

_____

_____

_____

_____

_____

_____

_____

_____

Although we may learn that vulnerability sets us up to be hurt, the Father asks that we present ourselves with all our walls and defenses down, trusting that he is with us, that he knows us, loves us, and enjoys us.

DON'T LEAVE ME

Even if my father and mother abandon me,
the LORD will hold me close.
—King David, Psalm 27:10 (NLT)

Abandonment is one of the worst feelings anyone can experience. When you were very little, did you ever lose sight of your mother or father in a store or public place? Remember how you felt? I do.

I (Jerry) was just a little guy, and I was with my mother in a clothing store. For just a few seconds—it felt like forever—I couldn't find her. I can still remember the panic that came over me, and my relief when we were reunited.

As a child, my father was unable to connect with me emotionally due to his own wounds. The sense of connectedness just wasn't there. In addition, my mother's childhood wounds resulted in her drawing on my emotions as a child rather than providing nurture and affection; instead of giving to me, she was taking from me.

Other incidents also contributed to my core fear of abandonment. When I was three or four years old, I found myself lying in a hospital crib with a surgery scheduled for the following day. My parents weren't there in the room, and I felt scared and alone. Another time, when I was about six, a terrible car crash occurred in front of our house, and a woman was killed. I feared the same thing could also happen to my parents, and then I would be alone. I can still picture these events in my mind today—but they don't have the power they once had. The memories are part of my story, but the gaping wounds have been healed.

Some sense of abandonment is likely to lie at our core. When we enter this world, we are already separated from God our Creator due to sin, and we begin the process of being reconciled and restored to him. In general, whenever a child—from infancy (and even prenatally) to adolescence—does not *feel* the love that is needed, he or she will experience some degree of abandonment, separateness, not belonging, or rejection.

We all understand that it is not possible for a parent to totally shield a child from such painful occurrences. However, it is critical for a parent to recognize when they happen and provide greater measures of the love, affectionate touch, sense of security, and belonging that will keep most of the child's abandonment issues in check.

When a child starts to experience feelings of abandonment—even as an infant—something starts to happen. The child begins to develop strong defense mechanisms to avoid the terrible pain. And in many cases, that child will have difficulty feeling the full range of emotions as an adult.

This core wound of emotional abandonment can create significant problems in close relationships, especially marriage. Some individuals are walled off while others may be needy and self-focused. In both cases, it is difficult to feel and communicate emotions.

To add salt to the wound, people with abandonment and rejection issues often abandon and reject themselves. Ouch! But it's true: we often "parent ourselves the way we were parented." So if physical and/or emotional abandonment occurred as a child, we avoid the pain by closing off or deadening a part of our emotions. Part of us gets fragmented and splits off from our core identity—and it is a part we need. We were never designed to live with any part of ourselves disconnected or shut away.

Thankfully, God wants all of our heart, and he will pursue us until we partner with him to "bring that part home."

Recently, I (Denise) had an unexpected experience of abandonment. It happened last year when my father died. He was ninety years old, he was failing, and we were prepared to say good-bye. At least, that is what we thought.

There was a surreal moment as we left the church and walked behind the casket toward the hearse. The pallbearers lifted the casket into the hearse and stepped back. An instant later, as my family members and I stood there at the end of the sidewalk, the hearse pulled away from the curb. Just as quickly, my heart sank into my stomach and I started sobbing. I felt these words screaming inside me: "He left me. He drove away. He isn't coming back." Two of his grandsons were right behind me and were crying too. I saw the same look on my sisters' faces as the stark reality hit home. Our hearts cried in unison, "Don't leave me."

You see, this was a moment where many of us were connecting with our own deep feelings of abandonment. Of course there was grief over the loss of our father, grandfather, brother. But the way it happened triggered something much deeper.

If you believe this wound of abandonment and rejection is still alive in you, then the first step to healing is to recognize and acknowledge that it exists. You must own the wound: "It really happened to me, and it matters." Ask God to open up the lost and abandoned parts in you that need to be found—to show you more about your childhood and what may have caused this core wound, and allow you to get in touch with the fear, hurt, and loss from abandonment.

Along the healing journey, it may be helpful for you to share your story with someone who can listen and understand. Many have found help connecting to their hearts through movies, music, or stories. It is absolutely critical for us to emotionally identify with our wound and meet God in our grief. God likes to go after lost things (see Luke 15). He grieves over our abandonment and what it has cost us. Since his love pushes out the fear, his plan is not only to find the missing part but also to fill it to capacity with his love.

PRAYER

Father, thank you for sending your Son to make a way for me to be connected to you. Thank you that I don't have to live a life—both now and in the life to come—where I am separated from you. But Lord, there are still places in me that need to feel more secure, places that make it more difficult for me to fully rest. I am willing to trust you with every part of me—even those parts I've stuffed away and abandoned. I want to be whole, and I don't want any part of me to be driven by fear. I know I never have to say to you, "Don't leave me," because you never have left me and you never will. Bring more healing to my heart so I can fully live from this place of being found by you.

THOUGHTS AND REFLECTIONS

He is a Father who comes alongside me and puts his arm around me, so I don't have to feel lonely or afraid. He is walking hand in hand with me, protecting me and standing up for me. I am not alone.

SHIELDS UP: THE WAYS WE PROTECT OURSELVES

The trouble with steeling yourself against the harshness of reality is that the same steel that secures your life against being destroyed secures your life also against being opened up and transformed.
—*Frederick Buechner*

Children come into this world with physical *and* emotional needs. Although the physical needs may be met, often many of the emotional needs are not. These emotional needs are not optional; they are essential to the healthy development of children as they progress and mature.

What happens when these needs are not met? How does a child deal with the pain of feeling rejected, neglected, or emotionally abandoned? These feelings in a child originate from parents who are well meaning but unavailable emotionally, as well as from parents and others who are overtly abusive. When children do not receive the necessary nurture and affection God designed them to receive, they develop difficulties in trusting others later in life—including God. In more and more families, children are expected to meet the needs of the parents while their own needs go unmet. And since children do not know what to do with the tremendous emotional pain of unmet needs, they learn to survive by developing defense mechanisms to protect themselves.

Unfortunately, we do not outgrow the defense mechanisms we needed as children. Instead, we carry them into adulthood and into our relationships. These defenses keep the unreleased pain of the past stuffed down inside us. What helped us survive as children—what was even provided by God for a helpless child—will no longer work in our favor as adults.

PRAYER FOR THE JOURNEY

As we begin Week Seven, we surrender our defensive walls of protection as we pray.

Father, I need your help. I know I have developed ways to protect myself from pain, especially pain that started long ago. I need you to show me the ways in which I have done this. Although I am uneasy and even fearful of opening this door, I want to live from the place of the "abundant life" your Son came to give me (John 10:10). As you expose the ways I have learned to protect myself, please give me the grace to reject my self-made shields and mechanisms.

I invite you in to defend and protect me. I ask you to make me weak with a godly weakness so I can live from your strength. Lord, I ask you to make me defenseless in my own ability, such that you can truly be my defense. And I tell you that I am willing to feel what you would have me feel—no more and no less than you say is necessary. I am willing, by your grace, to be emotionally honest, transparent, and vulnerable before you and before others who you say are trustworthy.

PLACING GOD'S ARMOR OVER OUR WALLS

*Only when you know in your deepest being
that you are intimately loved,
can you face the dark voices of the enemy
without being seduced by them.*
—Henri Nouwen

Normally, every day Denise and I place the "armor of God" upon ourselves for protection from evil. Our "armor" prayer is based on the words of Ephesians 6:10–17:

> Finally, be strong in the Lord and in his mighty power. Put on the full armor of God, so that you can take your stand against the devil's schemes. For our struggle is not against flesh and blood, but against the rulers, against the authorities, against the powers of this dark world and against the spiritual forces of evil in the heavenly realms. Therefore put on the full armor of God, so that when the day of evil comes, you may be able to stand your ground, and after you have done everything, to stand.
>
> Stand firm then, with the belt of truth buckled around your waist, with the breastplate of righteousness in place, and with your feet fitted with the readiness that comes from the gospel of peace. In addition to all this, take up the shield of faith, with which you can extinguish

all the flaming arrows of the evil one. Take the helmet of salvation and the sword of the Spirit, which is the word of God.

Here's where it gets tricky, though: I can pray this prayer thinking I'm putting God's armor directly on myself when in fact I'm placing it on top of something that is already in place—my own defensive armor.

The self-protective mechanisms we acquired in childhood, necessary back then to help us handle our hurts, are typically carried into our adulthood. We may think we are trusting God, but on deeper self-examination we find we are really trusting more in ourselves and our own means of self-protection.

For example, when I am deeply hurt in a relationship, I may respond by telling myself, "It wasn't that bad" or "People hurt people all the time. I just need to move on."

Years ago I used this type of self-protection—called *minimization*—to limit the pain I felt. By enabling me to control my emotions, minimization kept me from running to the heart of God for his help with my deep hurt.

I also erected a wall around my heart as a child so I wouldn't get hurt deeply in the future. I did this in various ways. One was to cut myself off emotionally (and sometimes physically) from the person who hurt me rather than working through the hurt with God. I also made internal decisions, or *vows*—"I'll never be angry," "I'll never let you know I'm hurting," and so on—to protect myself from painful emotions. I continued to rely on the armor of self-protection into my adult life, unaware that I was doing so.

If you, like me, regularly pray God's armor upon yourself, ask God to show you how you're using it. Are you truly putting it on over *yourself*—or over your *walls*, your own means of self-protection?

God wants to be our defense. He wants to be the one in whom we trust. Our own means of protecting ourselves is really no protection from evil at all. Our walls only become stronger and will hinder our hearts even more when evil comes our way. Only in our personal weakness—only when we give up our self-protection—can we experience God's strength (2 Cor. 12:9).

PRAYER

Lord Jesus, you are both the Lamb of God and the Lion of Judah. A loving father not only loves and cares for his children, but he will also fight on their behalf when they are threatened. That is how you are, Father. You are the lover and the defender of my heart. Please help me not only to know but also to feel and experience this reality. Help me to lay down any self-protection I have used. I need you to be both the Lion and the Lamb in my life.

THOUGHTS AND REFLECTIONS

What helped us to survive as children—what was even provided by God for a helpless child—will no longer work in our favor as adults.

TURN UP THE LIGHT IN MY HEART

*If we conceal our wounds out of fear and shame,
our inner darkness can neither be illuminated
nor become a light for others.*
—Brennan Manning

We were in the last week of our vacation in the Florida panhandle when we found out that a storm named Karen was forming in the Gulf of Mexico. Springing up from nowhere, it was potentially tracking our way—if not the eye, then the storm's east side, with its heavy rains and tornadoes.

We were extra tired this particular year, and we desperately needed a life-and-breath-giving break. I could not believe Karen might hamper that.

As it turned out, Karen became a nonevent except for a day and night of heavy, sideways downpours. But this is the awesome part: the next morning, after the storm had cleared, a gigantic rainbow lit the sky. At first we saw only a part of it, but when we got right up to the window, we saw the whole expanse, arching high across the heavens from the Gulf to the bayside of the island. It blazed away in brilliant color for at least twenty minutes. We took plenty of pictures!

The rainbow brought us a deep feeling of hope—hope that, like this storm, the other storms in our lives would come to an end. There would be a new day. Life. Hope. Breath. Connection. I (Denise) prayed that the Lord was extending the olive branch to me and to us. He had sent a rainbow, and with it, a promise—of life, of a new day, as in the story of Noah.

Fast-forward one month. I was sitting at my Mac editing our beach photos when I received an awesome surprise. There on the picture of the full rainbow was something we had not seen—a double rainbow. And not just a partial one but one that followed the entire arch of the first. Catch this—it wasn't until I added more brightness that the second rainbow was exposed.

PRAYER

Father God, turn up the light in my heart and let the increased brightness reveal you right there with me, even when I do not know you are there.

THOUGHTS AND REFLECTIONS

_____
_____
_____
_____
_____
_____
_____
_____
_____
_____
_____
_____
_____
_____
_____
_____
_____
_____
_____
_____
_____
_____
_____
_____
_____
_____
_____
_____
_____

I stand on the truth that no matter how dark things become, my Father will never leave or abandon me.

BREAKING FREE

To find God, you must look with all your heart.
To remain present to God, you must remain present to your heart.
To hear his voice, you must listen with your heart.
To love him, you must love with your heart.
You cannot be the person God meant you to be,
and you cannot live the life he meant you to live,
unless you live from the heart.
—John Eldredge

Be diligent in prayer. That is an important rule when it comes to healing our brokenness and getting free from our bondages.

But when will the breakthrough come for our hearts? Many of us have been hit by difficult life situations that have affected our inner world greatly. Whether it was the divorce of our parents, abuse or dysfunction in our home, or bullying at school, events and circumstances in our childhood play a key role in how we live as adults. Some of us have not even realized that our heart and emotions got run over by a Mack truck.

Consider the world's response if you were actually hit, physically, by a truck. You would be first in the ICU, then the step-down unit, then rehabilitation. You would have visitors, and flowers, and get-well-soon cards. It would take a while—maybe quite a while—for you to get back on your feet again.

Now imagine it is your heart that was run over. Where is all the support? Where are your cheerleaders who never give up on you? If you were in the hospital, nobody would say, "Hey, get over it. Rub some dirt in it and go on." So why do we do this for wounds on the inside?

Moreover, if it takes longer to heal our hearts than our bodies, how long are we going to pursue healing? If we see a counselor twice, or go to the altar a few times, or attend a small group for six weeks, or petition God for a season of time, and we don't experience the change we desire, do we just give up in hopelessness?

It is so much harder to be diligent with our emotional recovery because the wounds are on the inside.

We want to encourage you: God does not waste a single step in your pursuit of healing and freedom. Every prayer goes in the bowl that will be tipped in God's appointed time. Every tear will be saved in his bottle and recorded in his book (Ps. 56:8). Tears of pain. Tears of shame. Tears of anger. Tears of loneliness. Tears of grief. Every tear is collected by God.

Are our screams—silent or expressed—prayers to God? Does he hear those, too? Do our desperate, angry prayers count? *Yes*—an emphatic *YES*. We have seen this in our counseling sessions time and again. You don't have to cry for the right reasons—it counts simply that you cry. You don't have to pray eloquently—it counts. You don't even have to use words—it counts. It counts because God cares, and he knows that every cry to him is a hit against the enemy, who wants to keep us in bondage.

As those hits mount, the strongholds of shame, fear, depression, guilt, anger, and insecurity start losing their grip on us. A stronghold is a feeling or condition we have to fight to overcome. Envision a wrecking ball demolishing a concrete wall. The ball hits the wall several times with minimal visible progress. If the operator didn't know better, he would quit and look to plan B. But the wrecking ball, plan A, is still the one to complete the job. Maybe it takes fifteen hits before the operator starts to see cracks. Another five, ten, or twenty hits and the cracks become wider and pieces of concrete begin breaking away. On the fortieth hit the wall falls down.

This is how prayer and perseverance work, even when we feel that nothing is happening. Emotional healing takes time. It is a journey. But God is with us, right next to us. Listen closely to his whisper: "Do not faint and grow weary, my child, for the walls—they're coming down!"

PRAYER

Lord Jesus, thank you that you came to heal my broken heart and set me free. Thank you that you don't see internal wounds differently than external wounds. You just want me to be whole. I bring my heart to you and invite you to do whatever is needed to bring down the strongholds that have been established in my life. Help me to trust you and to extend the same grace to myself that you extend to me in this healing process. Though demolishing strongholds can be messy, you will not leave me in the rubble. You plan to restore my heart that I might truly live.

THOUGHTS AND REFLECTIONS

I realize that the healing process is hard work, but I am willing to say yes to the journey and step into it.

PIECE BY PIECE

God uses broken things. It takes broken soil to produce a crop,
broken clouds to give rain, broken grain to give bread, broken
bread to give strength. It is the broken alabaster box that gives
forth perfume. It is Peter, weeping bitterly, who returns to
greater power than ever.
—*Vance Hayner*

Unity is important to Jesus. On the very night he was betrayed, he prayed to the Father that his disciples (including us) would be one, as he and his Father are one. We commonly think of this oneness in a corporate sense—unity with one another. This is crucial and at the heart of the Scriptures. In *The Message*, the phrase "that they may be one" (John 17:21) is translated, "that all of them become one heart and mind."

However, in order for us to become of one heart and mind with one another, we must be of one heart and mind within ourselves. The more fragmented we are in our souls—our mind, will, and emotions—the more fragmented we will also live as a corporate body.

Most, if not all of us, are fragmented to some degree. It's the result of simply being born into a fallen world. Yet this fragmentation can vary considerably from one individual to another. That makes sense when someone has experienced severe abuse. But what about the person who has no history of overt abuse but who experienced a lack of effective nurturing in childhood? Or the person who grew up with passive or emotionally unavailable parents, or parents who were too busy to give their personal attention? In such circumstances fragmentation is not as easily identified or understood. But the broken pieces are still there inside.

The adult may struggle to connect with others and with God. He may have moments when he senses a level of closeness, but most of the time he lives emotionally and spiritually distant, from the outside looking in. She may revert to childish ways—slamming doors, throwing things, giving the silent treatment, or demanding her way. The man or woman may feel a common cry of exasperation on the inside: "Lord, there must be more. I feel broken somewhere inside." He or she may feel empty, invisible: "Can someone just hear me?" "Will someone listen to me?" "Does anyone even care about me?"

Sarah Dessen, in her book, *What Happened to Goodbye*, accurately describes the difficulty we face when we try to heal the breaks in our soul. *"It was like when you ripped a piece of paper into two: no matter how you tried, the seams never fit exactly right again. It was what you couldn't see, those tiniest of pieces, that were lost in the severing, and their absence kept everything from being complete."*[4]

Fragmentation can exist in even the most conscientious and active Christians, and many times those around them are unaware. But Father God knows, and he does not want us to live this way. He invites us to partner with him in the revealing and healing of our fragmented souls.

Now it is your turn to ask the Holy Spirit to show you more about your past. He may reveal a time in your life when, inside yourself, you began to "divide." Maybe you shut down your heart because you got hurt or were afraid. Or you became self-sufficient or decided to guard your heart. Or you began to feel you didn't measure up—you felt worthless, unaccepted, unwanted, alone, insignificant, or unloved.

Any or all of these will create disunity within a person. If the Holy Spirit brings such things from our past to the forefront, then we know and trust that what he reveals, he heals. And he heals for the ultimate purpose of oneness with him, which then overflows to others and to our world.

After all, that we would be one was Jesus's prayer.

PRAYER

Abba Father, I want to be whole. I want the fullness of your glory to shine through me. I know you can even shine through broken pieces. I don't have to be totally whole for you to love me and be with me. In this process, I trust you, and I believe that you are there to pick me up, even when I feel alone and abandoned. That you will always love me and take care of me. And as my Father, you'll always stay right by my side. No matter what.

THOUGHTS AND REFLECTIONS

_____

_____

_____

_____

_____

_____

_____

_____

_____

_____

_____

_____

_____

_____

_____

_____

_____

_____

_____

_____

_____

_____

_____

_____

_____

_____

_____

_____

I desperately need God to come into my fragmented heart and heal what was lost or damaged. Ironically, these same wounds have caused me to protect my heart and my emotions from even trusting that God will do this.

HIDING FROM LOVE

I am shielded in my armor,
Hiding in my room, safe within my womb.
I touch no one and no one touches me.
I am a rock; I am an island.
And a rock feels no pain,
And an island never cries.
—Paul Simon, "I Am a Rock"
Used by permission

"More power to the shields! Take it from life support!" That's the command from the Star Trek captain in the midst of an enemy attack. Pretty profound when you think about it. When we put up our guard, our shield, our fortified walls, then the energy to keep them in place has to come from somewhere. It takes emotional vigor to keep our heart safe behind our walls. We steel ourselves to keep our life support at acceptable levels. But we are in a battle—a battle for our very lives.

We like to tell a story we heard from Judith MacNutt which we call "The Message of the Daisies."[5] It is about a little man who was fearful around people—afraid that if they really knew him, they wouldn't like him. So he built a small wall around himself, so no one could see all of him. The wall was only up to his waist, but it made the man feel safer now, a little less vulnerable. After a while, it even felt like the wall was part of him.

As time went on, the man built the wall higher and higher until it was over his head and no one could see him. The man felt comfortable being alone. Now no one could hurt or reject or shame him. It was nice not to worry about that any more.

But after a while, when he heard the sounds of laughter and play, he felt very lonely.

One day someone threw a daisy over his wall. It was so beautiful—but it had come from outside. No flowers grew inside his wall, nor was there any laughter or love or joy. Now the man longed to get out of his fortress, but he didn't know how. He cried out to God, "Lord, please help me take down this wall I have built around my heart. I didn't realize that when I shut down my heart, I shut you out too."

The Father heard and lovingly responded. He and the little man sat down together and began looking at the man's past, from the womb, to the infant, to the toddler, preschooler, elementary school child, and adolescent. They went through some of the stories of the man's childhood and the negative impact each had on the little boy.

For the first time the little man allowed himself to feel the pain and fear he had stuffed all his life. Through this journey back to his childhood, God became a Father to him. He felt loved for the first time in his life. And when he saw the love and affection for him in the Father's eyes, he began to see himself the way the Father saw him. He overflowed with love and joy.

The story concludes with the little man running down the street throwing daisies over all the walls. He was no longer hiding from love.

When asked which defense mechanisms a client of ours used in his life, the client suddenly started singing the lyrics to Paul Simon's famous song "I Am a Rock": "I am a rock; I am an island. And a rock feels no pain, and an island never cries." Whoa! We call this defense mechanism *self-sufficiency* and *self-reliance*—and the man lived from this position. How well does that work in relationships? Not very well at all. Like others, the man learned at an early age how to survive but never how to live.

One young man, severely physically abused as a boy, remembers lying in bed at night, afraid that monsters would come and get him (like his dad did when he was angry). He followed rigid rules of checking and rechecking all the monsters' potential hiding places. After his routine, he would crawl in bed and cover up with the blankets up to his nose. He felt safe then—the monsters could not get him.

In the summer it got pretty hot upstairs in his bedroom, so he would make up new rules for the monsters: "Okay, from now on it is safe to have one leg out from under the covers." The deals with the monsters continued as the heat of summer lingered. By the time fall came around, the boy had quite a collection of defense mechanisms in his tool chest: Denial, to avoid his feelings by minimizing their existence. Pretending and fantasizing, to deaden the reality of his pain. Dissociation, "zoning out," to escape from his feelings. Emotional insulation, to close off his heart so he didn't have to feel. Whatever the fears were that came with the monsters in his room, they never compared with the fear when the boy's father came up to his room at night, drunk.

We all have many reasons why we learned to hide our hearts from being hurt. And because we often get hurt in love, we learned to hide from love as well. The Father is now inviting us to come out of hiding. We will have to begin to feel again—feel the truth of what really happened to us.

We may ask, "Why do I have to look at the past? Why go through all that again?"

Because we never went all the way through the pain the first time.

We never expressed our feelings at the crucial times—feelings that belonged there. One client summed it up perfectly: "My disease was a hole in my soul. The child inside me was directing my life and my heart. I had to feel his pain and grieve my losses to be healed."

It's worth repeating: Feel it to heal it. Grieve it to leave it.

PRAYER

Father God, I realize that I still guard my heart, especially with those closest to me—and even with you. I have been afraid to be totally vulnerable in order to protect myself from hurt, rejection, and abandonment. Father, I need you to be my safe place. I am willing to trust you with my heart. I'm willing to walk with you back through the rooms of my past—even into the room with the monsters. I am willing to feel what you feel about these broken places in me so that I can ultimately be healed by you.

THOUGHTS AND REFLECTIONS

To experience healing from my emotional wounds, I must address the "shields" that guard my heart—not only from being hurt, but also from being fully engaged and alive.

SHAME AND THE LIES WE BELIEVE

I have never known who I really was because my whole life
I have been wearing a mask, performing for and trying to
please others. My mother even made me dress up with full
makeup and my hair done to go to the mailbox—because
"you never know if someone will see you."
—A Teen Recovering from Anorexia

Healthy shame (true guilt) allows us to feel pain and sorrow when we violate God-designed ways of loving him, ourselves, and others. Toxic, destructive shame is much different. It is one of the most prevalent and harmful issues that we address in counseling. Toxic shame robs us of the life that the Father intends us to experience. It interferes with our living passionately as lovers of God and our fellow humans.

Toxic shame exacts an exorbitant price in our lives. It costs us love, friendships, acceptance, hope, and connectedness. Worst of all, it robs us of an intimate relationship with God. Shame causes us to see the Father through distorted lenses and thus inhibits us from receiving the love he has for us. Instead of enjoying simply *being* with God as the overflow of a love relationship with him, we wind up *performing* for God in order to please him and earn his love.

PRAYER FOR THE JOURNEY

As you begin Week Eight, offer the Father your heart and pray with us:

Father, I want to be whole. I want to view myself the way you view me and love myself the way you love me. Lord, if there is any destructive, toxic shame within me that hinders my ability to do so, I ask you to reveal it to me. I ask this so that I can ultimately walk in the freedom you desired for me when you sent your Son, Jesus, to restore all things—including me.

I want to be free of the lies that still affect me and influence my ability to love you, myself, and others. And I know that if you reveal this type of shame in me, it is already your plan to ultimately heal me from its effects. Please have your way in me. Thank you for your love.

CONTROL POINTS TO FEAR

We ask ourselves, "Who am I to be brilliant, gorgeous,
talented or fabulous?" Actually, who are you not to be?
You are a child of God. Your playing small doesn't serve the
world. There's nothing enlightened about shrinking so that
other people won't feel insecure around you.
We were born to manifest the glory of God that is within us.
. . . And as we are liberated from our own fear, our presence
automatically liberates others.
—John Eldredge

When we schedule an individual or a couple for intensive counseling, we use a self-assessment form to help them and us understand more about why they are seeking help. This form lists various statements under such headings as Fear, Assert Control, Resist Control, and Flee Intimacy, to name a few. The client selects any statements that apply. Through this form, as well as by other means, we have learned that many people misunderstand the word *fear*.

What first comes to mind when you think of that word? Someone who is anxious about something, like having to speak in front of an audience? Maybe snakes or spiders make you shudder, or the thought of flying. There are a multitude of possibilities, both real and imagined, for feeling apprehensive. But guess who some of the most fearful people are: those who seem to be the most in control.

Let's unpack this further and look at fear from another viewpoint. A term that has received a lot of attention in counseling and self-help circles is *codependency*. Although this word can have a multitude of meanings, it usually refers to someone who is involved in one or more relationships where he or she is controlled or manipulated by the needs of the other person. The codependent may have an unhealthy fear of confronting that person and thus remains in more of a one-way relationship. The fear or anxiety in a codependent person tends to be easier to detect and understand; someone might say this type of person lacks the backbone to stand up for him- or herself.

But what about the other person in that type of relationship? Often that person would be termed a *counterdependent*, or one who dominates or controls the codependent. The counterdependent personality is the strong one in the relationship, exercising subtle or overt power over the other person. But is this person also operating from a base of fear? Although the fear looks quite different, the answer is unequivocally yes.

For example, if I have a need to be in control—of you, of my surroundings, of my life in general—I cannot rest. Something deep within me must make sure things stay in control, and the fear—sometimes buried very deep—cannot tolerate it when things are not in control. I may use strength or power, or self-sufficiency and self-reliance (pride), but it is really only a means to cover up my fear and insecurity. I cannot trust others or God, another by-product of fear. Interestingly, what is actually working right alongside this hidden fear is inferiority and low self-esteem (toxic shame).

Back to the self-assessment form we mentioned earlier. When we see high numbers in such categories as Assert Control, Resist Control, and Flee Intimacy, we will help our client realize that fear is involved. We will work together at uncovering and inviting God to heal the root of this fear.

We often need to remind our clients and ourselves that if fear is actively involved in our lives—it usually shows up in our most intimate relationships—then most likely there is a "love deficit" within. Why? Because "there is no room in love for fear. Well-formed love banishes fear. Since fear is crippling, a fearful life—fear of death, fear of judgment—is one not yet fully formed in love" (1 John 4:18 MSG).

PRAYER

Father, show me where fear is having an influence in my life—in my heart Open the "eyes of my heart" to see what you see. And help me to rest in the truth that when you reveal things that are out of agreement with your heart, it is not because you want to find something wrong with me. You do it because you love me and want me to be free. As you reveal, please heal me, Father, and eradicate all ungodly fear in me by your pursuing and unending love.

THOUGHTS AND REFLECTIONS

I want to hate the mask I wear to cover my shame and my fears. I need the love of God and others to reach my heart so it is not my mask that receives the love.

YOU ARE MY LIONEL

*There is a desire within each of us, in the deep center of
ourselves that we call our heart. We were born with it, it is
never completely satisfied, and it never dies. We are often
unaware of it, but it is always awake. . . . Our true identity,
our reason for being, is to be found in this desire.*
—Gerald May

Have you seen the powerful movie *The King's Speech*? The story is of the
man who reluctantly assumed the British throne as King George VI.
He suffered with a dreadful stammer that seemingly made him unfit to
be king. But through the help and friendship of an unorthodox speech
therapist named Lionel, the king was able to find his voice and become
worthy of the throne.

At the time this movie was hitting the theaters, we had been working
with a client for several months. You met him a couple chapters ago. As
a boy, he had lived in fear of the night and monsters in his room, but his
greater fear was of the emotional and verbal abuse he received from his
father. He became hypervigilant in the hope of predicting when the next
attack would come. He knew full well that no warning was ever enough
to avoid the drama and trauma and the words that cut him to his core.

Fast-forward forty years. Now the grown man was sitting in our
counseling office. He was one year into working with us to heal the trau-

ma from his childhood that affected his current relationships, including his connection with Father God. The man handed us two tickets to *The King's Speech* and asked us to call him after we saw the film. There was something he wanted to share with us that we would only understand after we saw the movie.

Two weeks later we watched the movie, and then we called the man. With a break in his voice, he whispered, "You are my Lionel. You gave me a voice. You believed in me. You cared."

We were undone by such a heart-stopping sentiment. What had happened with this man was God. It was God's heart for him. No one wanted him to have a voice more than God did. The rules he learned in his dysfunctional family—don't talk, don't feel, don't trust—were rewritten by Father God:

"I have given you a voice."

"I have given you a heart that is made to feel."

"I have made you to trust so that you can hold your heart open to love."

To be given a voice is not to constantly talk. Sometimes the greatest voice we have is when we choose to be silent. When Jesus stood before Pilate, he never opened his mouth, but his heart cry could be heard throughout the heavens. When we have a voice, we can learn when to speak and when to listen. Christ's silence was not because of fear or shame or from walling off his heart. Like him, we can choose silence and rest because "God knows." God is our defense. God hears our heart even when no sound comes from our lips.

If there is someone in your life who is your Lionel, you are blessed. If not, then maybe you could become your own Lionel. Listen to the voice God has put inside you. Ask for his direction on how to be a voice, have a voice, and hear his voice.

PRAYER

Father God, you say in your Word that if I call to you, you will answer me and show me great and unsearchable things—things I do not know (Jer. 33:3). It was you who created me with a voice so I could call out to you, praise you, and freely share your heart with others. But Lord, things have happened that have hindered the voice that you gave me. I invite you to restore everything that you intended for me to have when you created me, and that includes my voice. Moses felt his voice was inadequate to speak to Pharaoh on your behalf, yet ultimately he used his voice with authority; grant me that same freedom and authority with the voice you have given me.

THOUGHTS AND REFLECTIONS

Children who grow up in dysfunctional, shame-based families learn three cardinal rules. Don't talk. Don't feel. Don't trust.

THAT'S NOT WHAT
IT MEANS

*The secret killer of innovation is shame. You can't measure it,
but it is there. Every time someone holds back on a new idea,
fails to give their . . . much needed feedback, and is afraid to
speak up in front of [others], you can be sure shame plays a part.
That deep fear we all have of being wrong, of being belittled
and of feeling less than, is what stops us from taking the
very risks required to move . . . forward.*
—Brene Brown

Some years ago we had a speaker conduct a weekend conference on destructive, toxic shame. While finishing his final talk, he passed out cards that were about six by six inches, and on these cards were the words "That's Not What It Means." The cards were to help us remember that whenever we were confronted with a potential shame message, we should avoid jumping to a negative conclusion.

You see, toxic shame has more to do with our core identity and our negative beliefs about ourselves than with anything we have actually done or not done. Yes, our wrong actions (or lack of actions) can cause us to feel ashamed—a better word would be "guilty"—but actions can be addressed and eventually rectified. We can seek to make amends and pursue reconciliation with the one we have hurt or offended. And even if that cannot be achieved, we can ask for and receive forgiveness from God.

Toxic shame, on the other hand, gives us no way out. It doesn't just say, "You really messed up"; it says, "You *are* messed up." It doesn't just say, "That was a stupid thing you just did"; it says, "You *are* stupid." Toxic shame attacks who you are, not just what you do.

The terrible problem with toxic shame is that those who are under its sway experience much of life through its filter. When someone tries to share something corrective in nature with such a person, he will probably have a very difficult time receiving it the right way. He may end up either berating himself or the other person, even if he only does so internally. Or maybe the next time he will work extra hard to be perfect so he doesn't have to face the possibility of looking inadequate or inferior. His toxic shame alarm screams, "AVOID SHAME AT ALL COST."

But the worst damage from toxic shame comes in relationships. We cannot even count the number of terrible marital conflicts we have seen as counselors that could have been avoided had one or both spouses simply believed the words "That's Not What It Means." For example, a wife feels hurt from her husband's perceived lack of attention and interest in her when he calls to say he won't be home for dinner. Based on that experience—especially when it occurs more than once—she then says to herself, "I'm not attractive or desirable. I'm not special. He really doesn't care about me or my needs."

Or a husband feels hurt when his wife expresses concern that he doesn't spend enough time with the kids. From that experience he concludes, "I don't measure up. I'm not good enough. I can never do it good enough." In both of these situations, the assumptions made and the messages that are internalized are false. That's Not What It Means. In the first situation, the husband may feel stressed out over issues at work, and his anxiety interferes with his connecting with his wife in a loving way. In the second situation, the wife may be legitimately concerned over her husband's relationship with the kids. She hopes that by sharing her concern, a change may occur. Unhealthy reactions in these situations might range from shutting down and withdrawing to confronting and escalating, but the bottom line is that the real issue is no longer the issue—toxic shame has taken over and is controlling the interaction.

In my early years of marriage to Denise, I had a great deal of toxic shame, but I didn't know it. The core lies and shame within me prevented me from being emotionally honest with myself and with others—including Denise. As a result, our relationship suffered until I let God deal with my wounds and replace the core lies—the toxic shame—with his truth about me.

Now I don't have to fall into the trap like I did years ago, and I don't have to always think about that card, "That's Not What It Means," to help me avoid the toxic shame trap. I can give and receive more from a place of honesty and vulnerability, knowing that I am not perfect and never will be, and I don't have to force others to be that way either. Because of God's grace and his loving commitment to heal my heart of toxic shame, I know "What It Really Means" to love God, myself, and others—especially Denise.

PRAYER

Lord Jesus, show me if there are "shame filters" that interfere with my relationship with you and others. Help me see if there are lies about myself that I have accepted as true, and if so, give me the grace to allow you to do whatever is needed to reveal their origin. And Lord, replace these lies with your truth—how you see me and what you feel about me. Heal me, Jesus, from the effects of toxic shame, so I can be secure in whom you made me to be and thus live more from a place of rest—with you, with myself, and with others.

THOUGHTS AND REFLECTIONS

When we believe lies about ourselves and shame ourselves, it wars against God's very heart.

WHOSE VOICE DO YOU BELIEVE?

*When I was eight, the imposter, or false self, was born as
a defense against pain. The imposter within whispered,
"Brennan, don't ever be your real self anymore because nobody
likes you as you are. Invent a new self that everybody will
admire and nobody will know."*
—*Brennan Manning*

Are you aware of how many messages you listen to every day from the
radio station playing between your ears? The voice is not only your own
self-talk but also rehearsals of conversations, both real and perceived,
with your spouse, parents, children, boss, colleagues, friends, even the
check-out clerk at the store. The list of voices goes on and on.

Sometimes negative, critical, or shaming messages from your past
bleed into your airwaves—familiar messages you internalized from your
family of origin and other significant people in your life. Your childhood
has a profound impact on the quality of messages you produce in your
internal dialogue. The more shame, guilt, rejection, neglect, and abuse
you experienced growing up, the more skewed your reception of positive
and affirming messages will be.

One of our counseling professors, Gary Moon, liked to use the anal-
ogy of a radio station as the vehicle for discerning the voice of God versus

that of the enemy.⁶ Let's listen in for a minute to the messages from the two "talk radio" hosts, as we envision them, and the different spin of each.

WGOD	WLIE
Cohosted by Father, Son, and Spirit	*Cohosted by Enemy and Self*
Calls me by name, very personal	Points a finger at me, refers to me as "you" (how personal is that?)
Asks to be invited	Uninvited—crashes the party
Extends relationship to me	Extends the law, rules, and "shoulds and oughts"
Reassures me with his help	Creates fear, anxiety, and agitation about my choices
Corrects my course in love and shows me how to respond and be restored	Condemns and shames me so I feel alone, bad, or rejected, or determined to "power up" in order to gain control over shame
Teaches me honesty and vulnerability	Hands me a mask to hide behind so I can look good

Is WGOD too "easy listening" for you? Is WLIE more fitting with your personal beliefs and value system because you believe you must be hard on yourself (or so you won't think too highly of yourself)?

Put another way, when you bring your problems, struggles, and failures to God, what do you come away with? A solution? Enlightenment? Mercy? Conviction of a specific sin (versus a generalized "You are just bad")? Practical actions for the future? Encouragement? Reassurance that God is with you and will never leave you? Increased love, hope, and peace? Better understanding of and care for others? If so, you are listening to the Father heart of God.

However, if you hear screaming or loud volume, blame without mercy toward you or others, words that ascribe little worth, reminders of past failures; if you feel more confused, discouraged, hopeless, and deflated—

more critical of or angry with yourself, God, or others—then you are listening to station WLIE. Sometimes the enemy doesn't even bother with the broadcast when you can handle the negative self-talk all by yourself!

More than three hundred years ago, there lived a humble man known for his conversations with God while doing the dishes. His name was Brother Lawrence, and his writings in *The Practice of the Presence of God* have been shared throughout the centuries. He had what I would call a major shift in radio stations ten years after his salvation. He turned the dial from WLIE to WGOD. Why? Because he learned the secret; he learned to recognize the heart, the voice, and the love of the Father, who drew him into his heavenly embrace.

In *Practicing the Presence of God*, Brother Lawrence describes the lies he first believed during the first ten years of his walk with God. We have italicized them for emphasis in the next paragraph, and in some cases expanded on them in parentheses.

Lawrence *worried* that he *was not measuring up* with what God expected of him. He *couldn't forget his past (self-condemning)* and felt *tremendously guilty* over the amount of grace God extended to him (*i.e., he felt unworthy to receive good things from God*). He fell often (*"Loser!"*) and then would try hard to get up again (*"I promise to try harder next time"*). Sometimes he felt so *hopeless* about his failures that he thought he was on his way to hell (*judged and condemned*) for willfully offending God (*merciless self-judgment*). He was *afraid* there was no salvation for him; *he felt guilty, unworthy, and "too much" even for God.*

BUT GOD . . . because his very essence is love, he brought Brother Lawrence into rest with a profound inner peace. The lies, the Liar, and the negative self-talk were silenced. After those first ten years of condemnation, Brother Lawrence discovered God's true voice and his right-there-with-him presence. Lawrence still confessed his sins against his Father and King and asked him for forgiveness. But rather than punishment, Brother Lawrence experienced the opposite.

This King, Who is full of goodness and mercy, doesn't punish me. Rather, He embraces me lovingly and invites me to eat at His table. He serves me Himself and gives me the keys to His treasury, treating me as His favorite. He converses with me without mentioning my sins or my [asking for] forgiveness. My former habits are seemingly forgotten. Although I beg Him to do whatever He wishes with me, He does nothing but caress me.[7]

Now, that is a radio station the ears of my heart need to listen to. It is life giving. It is from the Giver of Life. Can you listen? Can you hear? Can you accept the Father's invitation to come and sit and stay awhile in the very presence of love? It may feel uncomfortable—even too good to be true. Yet that is the true gospel. Can you come into his rest today? Be embraced? Eat at his table? Be served by a Father who treats you as his favorite? Oh my!

Take some time today, this week, this lifetime to practice the presence of God. Then you will find that, somehow, even doing dishes can bring God-life to your heart.

PRAYER

Abba, how I need to hear your voice and not the voice of the Accuser. Reveal and remove all of the familiar voices that connect with the wounds of toxic shame and oppose your loving heart for me. Break the power of the Liar and the lies, and flood me with your truth. You say in your Word that your sheep hear and know your voice. I am yours, so help me to hear your voice and to reject anything else. I want to hear from, and be in agreement with, you and you alone.

THOUGHTS AND REFLECTIONS

_____

_____

_____

_____

_____

_____

_____

_____

_____

_____

_____

_____

_____

_____

_____

_____

_____

_____

_____

_____

_____

_____

_____

_____

_____

_____

I accept the Father's invitation to come and sit with him in the very presence of his love—even if it feels too good to be true.

EMBRACING THE FREEDOM TO FAIL

The paradox here is that the more we find we cannot do,
the more room there is for God to do.
In powerlessness lies our strength.
—Chip Dodd

When did failure get a bad name in your life? When did it stop being an obvious part of developing and learning, a normal part of life? When did failure stop being an expectation for growth and instead become something to avoid at all costs—like shame?

I (Denise) love picturing a baby's first steps. How exciting! How proud and privileged are those who are privy to this great scene. I can see the video rolling now: The baby begins to take steps along the edge of the couch, holding on for balance and dear life. Then, suddenly, a new thought, a spontaneous urge, a compulsion to let go and step away. One step—boom! —down on the bum, and a moment or two of wailing. Then time to get up and try again. A step—and still standing! The onlookers are ecstatic. "He took his first step." Baby's previous attempts that ended on the bum—they're forgotten. The "failures" don't even register; Mom and Dad are just in awe of that first step, excited about this moment of growth and development that will blossom exponentially and change their world. Baby's walking, and then running, creates a tremendous increase in their responsibilities to ensure protection and safety for their child. But who cares? *He took his first step!*

Looking back over my life, I can see how the Father was intimately and diligently working in the midst of my failures. I wish some of them were not part of my story, yet I learned many life lessons by failing—lessons I might not have learned otherwise.

I love the story of a man recounting all his mistakes and failures to his counselor. The counselor stops him and pulls out a sign for him to read: "The God Who Wastes Nothing."[8] God wastes nothing of our lives, and that includes our mistakes and failures. Of course there are often consequences to them, and we need to make amends when they injure others. But if we let our failures stop us, we will miss the opportunity to grow, learn, and enlarge. And we face an even greater loss: missing out on the freedom to run into the room of grace and experience a loving Father who keeps a record of our tears (Ps. 56:8), not our wrongs (1 Cor. 13:5). A Father who defines us by our adoption as his sons and daughters, not by our struggles and failures. If this Father of ours in heaven, who knows everything about us, does not define us by our struggles, then neither should we.

Moving toward the God who wastes nothing may take some action steps on your part as well as a few new choices. Here is a big one: dethroning your striving for perfection, as well as your performing to please others, and allowing vulnerability, honesty, and freedom to fail to take a front seat in your life. In doing so, may your story be transformed, your heart renewed, and your real self brought forth. May you discover that you offer a gift to the world when you embrace your failures. They are an unexpected ally in loving God and loving yourself.

PRAYER

Father, thank you that you do not expect me to be perfect. Thank you that you give me the freedom to fail, so I can know my own limitations, learn from my failures, and become even more dependent on you. Thank you that you are the God who wastes nothing. Let me rest in the security of your love and in whom you've made me to be.

THOUGHTS AND REFLECTIONS

I do not have to be perfect in order to be loved, because God loves me as I am—imperfect. This means that I am important even when I have rough edges in my life and when I make mistakes, even big ones. I can fail. I can stumble. God still says, "I love you!"

GOOD GRIEF: FROM SELF-FORGIVENESS TO SELF-ACCEPTANCE

The most important thing we ever hope for from God is
God Himself. Hope that He will be with us in our troubles.
Not necessarily for Him to take our troubles away,
but always to be there,
under us to hold us up, ahead of us to lead the way,
behind us to push us along, over us to keep an eye on us,
and in us to keep alive our hopes of getting beyond our troubles.
—Lewis Smedes

Loss is an inevitable part of life. At one time or another we all experience it. Our losses can either hinder our growth and destiny or help us move forward to fulfill them. In order for us to heal from our past wounds, we must be able to grieve over our losses. When we allow ourselves to feel sorrow or sadness as a result of a loss, we assign value to that loss. We are saying that it mattered.

Grieving losses, especially significant ones, is normal. If we learn as a child that it's better not to feel unpleasant feelings, and if we move on quickly when bad things happen, then we will maintain the same pattern as we get older. Consequently, our hearts will be adversely affected and remain unhealed.

Godly grieving of life's losses, on the other hand, leads to acceptance of ourselves, others, and our past. It also allows us to break free from unhealthy patterns of relating that are bound to unresolved pain. We must allow God access to every single room in our heart. Because it matters to him (and it should also matter to us), he will show us *why* it mattered—the cost we incurred. Then we can begin to grieve—and heal.

PRAYER FOR THE JOURNEY

As we begin Week Nine, we again take the risk of opening our hearts in vulnerability as we pray:

Lord Jesus, I want to be able to grieve what has also grieved your heart. I want to be able to live from a heart that is connected to you and to life, not simply step over things in my past that have been difficult and painful. You did not design me to stockpile losses, whether childhood losses or losses as an adult. You desire that I feel what you feel and that I work through my losses rather than sidestep them. I need your help in doing this. I need to know that you will be with me, helping me "grieve it to leave it."

I need your help in order to forgive others as well as myself, and come to a place not of resignation but of true acceptance. Lord, help me accept myself the way you accept me. Help me to truly love what you love—me.

GOD, DID IT MATTER?

The first thing Jesus promises is suffering. "I tell you . . . you will be weeping and wailing . . . and you will be sorrowful." But he calls these birth pains. And so, what seems a hindrance becomes a way; what seems an obstacle becomes a door; what seems a misfit becomes a cornerstone. Jesus changes our history from a random series of sad incidents and accidents into a constant opportunity for a change of heart.
—Henri Nouwen

Not all of the following questions will apply to you. But some will likely hit painfully close to home—the home you grew up in. The home you still carry with you inside. Lay them before God as you read.

> God, did it matter that I was conceived out of wedlock?
> That I was unwanted or the "wrong" sex?
> That I never met my biological dad until I was grown?
> That my parents didn't have a name picked out for me when I was born?

> Did it matter that I never heard "I love you" growing up?
> That my dad provided everything we needed but was never there for us?
> That my dad cheated on my mom?
> That my dad was silent and unemotional?

God, did it matter that my dad came to all my games but never said he was proud of me?

Did it matter that my mom needed me, confided in me, and sought comfort from me—that I was forced to be a little adult, mature and responsible, when I was supposed to just be a kid?

Did it matter that my dad kept pornography in the house where any child could find it?

That he would explode and then act like nothing happened?

That my mom wasn't a nurturer and I never bonded with her?

That my mom or dad never said, "I'm sorry," "I was wrong," or "Please forgive me?"

Did it matter that I was slapped in the face or that the spankings left marks?

That I never learned it was okay to cry?

That I never learned I can make mistakes, or say "I'm afraid," or say "No" when it is best for me to do so?

That I never knew I didn't have to be perfect or good to be loved?

That I was throttled with the law of shoulds and oughts and never experienced the freedom of love and grace.

God, did it matter that my father encouraged me to "sow some oats" before my wedding day?

Did it matter that my parents never came to my high school events, including my graduation?

That they never said anything to me if I stayed out all night or came home drunk?

Never modeled how to resolve conflict in relationship?

Gave me advice but never listened to my desires or tried to understand me?

God, did it matter that I never knew my needs matter and that *I* matter?

Did it matter that my parents divorced when I was little?
That Mom's boyfriend touched me sexually?
That I learned to keep secrets and not tell?
That my parents never helped me explore my uniqueness and place in the world?

Did it matter that I learned to wear a mask and perform in order to avoid rejection or shame?

God, would it matter if I had never been born?

Before you pray the closing prayer, take a few minutes and reflect on your childhood. What do you feel about the things that happened that should never have happened? What do you feel about the things that you needed to happen and that should have happened but never did? Do they matter to you? *Should* they matter to you? As you pray with us, ask Jesus to allow you to know and *feel* what he knows and feels about this question: *Did it matter?*

PRAYER

Lord Jesus, you were passionate during your ministry on the earth, and you are still passionate today. Your feelings concerning those who hurt your little ones is strong—and we who trust in you will always be your little ones. The impact of any sin committed against us, or by us, matters to you because it blocks the life you came to give.

Since your Father sent you to redeem us from sin and death and restore us to himself, we matter. Help me to take this truth deep within my soul and spirit. Just as a hurting child matters to me, how much more the hurts in my own life matter to you. Let me feel what you feel for this child within me, so I can grieve what is necessary for me to grieve.

THOUGHTS AND REFLECTIONS

In order for us to heal from our past wounds, we must be able to grieve over our losses.

UNSHAKEABLE FAITH IS FAITH THAT HAS BEEN SHAKEN

Is anyone crying for help?
GOD is listening, ready to rescue you.
If your heart is broken, you'll find GOD right there.
—Psalm 34:17–18 (MSG)

Some time ago, I (Denise) was given a round, white ceramic picture frame. The word "Believe" was inscribed on the bottom. I wasn't quite sure what to put in it until one day the perfect answer came.

As Jerry and I were walking along on the beach together, we noticed a small, round seed bouncing along ahead of us. Then it started "following" us. It was the strangest thing. It would get behind us, and then all of a sudden a gust of wind would come. There would be the seed again, rolling past us and getting ahead of us. It would roll and roll on the packed sand, always ending up with us. This went on for several minutes.

After a while, I remembered my picture frame and the gospel story of having "faith like a mustard seed" (Matt. 17:20). I picked up the seed, took it home, and placed it in the "Believe" picture frame. It was a nice touch on the side table of our living room.

One day while I was playing ball with Grace, our border collie, the ball bounced off her nose and went flying directly into the picture frame. The frame hit the floor and cracked on both sides. It wasn't the type of break that could be repaired, and I'm sure just about anyone else would have simply thrown it away. But the incident stopped me in my tracks. The broken frame . . . the "seed of faith" under the glass . . . the "Believe" inscription—suddenly they spoke to me very meaningfully of my life. Their message: Only faith that has been shaken can produce unshakeable faith. And godly brokenness can become a means to expand our capacity to hope, to believe, and to love.

PRAYER

Father, thank you that you are near when I, like the picture frame, am shaken by things around me. You are a good Father who doesn't run away from my brokenness; rather, you are close to me during those times (Ps. 34:18). Thank you that there is nothing that can separate me from you. Help me to always cry out to you in my brokenness and hold that small seed of faith in my heart. Though my faith may be shaken at times, you are unshakeable, and you are building an unshakeable faith in me.

THOUGHTS AND REFLECTIONS

_____
_____
_____
_____
_____
_____
_____
_____
_____
_____
_____
_____
_____
_____
_____
_____
_____
_____
_____
_____
_____
_____
_____
_____
_____
_____
_____
_____

I have hope that I can take all that I am and all that I have to God—the good and the bad—and he will keep on helping me grow more and more into his image.

PULL OVER OR KEEP ON DRIVING

Draw me, however unwilling, to make me willing;
draw me, slow-footed, to make me run.
—St. ·Bernard

I (Jerry) know myself well enough by now to realize that a significant shift in my emotions—whether toward anger, sadness, fear, or numbness—is a signal I need to heed. It's like a highway construction flagman directing me to pull over to the side until the emotional roadblock begins to clear. Do I always instantly heed the flagman? I wish I could say yes, but I'm pretty sure God wants me to tell you the truth.

More times than I want to admit, I ignore the signal and keep driving a little longer. Finally, though—due sometimes to my growing anxiety and sometimes to Denise's urging—I pull over and invite the Father into the emotions behind the roadblock. How? What works best for me is writing a letter to the Father and then allowing him to write back .

Once, after pouring out my heart to God about "running away from him rather than running to him," I stopped writing and just waited. After a brief time, I sensed a great deal of sadness, and tears began to come. God began sharing with me a loss I had grieved in the past which, without my realizing it, was still impacting me. Although the flagman of my emotions was signaling me, I had been pushing away the pain and grief.

Within a minute or two, I began to write what I sensed the Father speaking to my heart:

> It is not that you have not grieved your losses, but when some of them come back up again, you must allow yourself to acknowledge them. Your heart is dynamic, not static, and thus you will feel things that you have felt previously. When you do not allow this, you lose that part of your heart, and I do not want any part of your heart to be left behind.

God was reminding me of something I knew and even shared with others but did not necessarily always follow: that it is important to understand the dynamics that often surround our processing of pain and loss, especially when we feel we have already dealt with an issue. God also reminded me that even though I resisted opening up my heart, the Father continued to be available to me, standing at my heart's door, and was more than willing to respond to my invitation to enter the situation and help me. He didn't punish me for my resistance and my running, but he also didn't force his way in. Rather, he waited for me to yield to him, and as I did, he began to reconnect me both with my own heart and with his.

PRAYER

Father, you know me better than I know myself. You know when my heart needs to be cared for in a particular way. Help me recognize the signs of emotional and spiritual heart problems and choose to respond at those times. When I do—even if only for a few moments—I am choosing you and your ways. Help me see you for who you truly are and trust you with my pain, loss, and grief. I don't want to keep on "driving" when it is time to pull over.

THOUGHTS AND REFLECTIONS

I will not step over my heart when painful emotions come. I am willing to grieve it to leave it because I now realize that I can't fully heal what I cannot really feel.

JOURNEY OF BROKENNESS

*Our capacity for wholeheartedness can never be greater
than our willingness to be broken-hearted.
It means engaging with the world from a place
of vulnerability and worthiness.*
—*Brene Brown*

Several years ago the Lord showed me (Denise) a picture of my heart, and there were major cracks in it. Jesus was in white masonry clothes, standing right next to it. In one hand was a palette of mortar, and in the other was a trowel. He started taking the mortar and repairing all the major cracks in my heart and smoothing them over.

Some pieces of my heart lay shattered on the floor, too badly damaged to be repaired; brand-new parts were needed. Jesus applied large portions of mortar to those areas and created a new heart that was totally whole. I said, "Lord, that looks great, but cement becomes hardened, and I don't want a hard heart." He didn't say anything but took out his Bic lighter, flicked it, and set my heart on fire. I thought, "Great, he repaired my heart and set it on fire for him." What I didn't realize was that it was the fire of purification, and it would take me further on my journey of brokenness, vulnerability, and transformation.

Scripture speaks of aromas that are pleasing sacrifices to the Most High God. Is it any surprise that God would find our sacrifice of a broken heart pleasing to his nostrils? Psalm 51:17 states, "My sacrifice, O God, is a broken spirit; a broken and contrite heart you, God, will not despise." But what is a broken and contrite heart?

A broken heart can have many causes. It can be broken from sin or from an encounter with God (as in Isaiah 6:5, when Isaiah realized his insignificance and unholiness). It can be broken from wrestling with God for a blessing, as Jacob did in Genesis 32:22–32, or broken from circumstance or loss. I have experienced my share of brokenness, *especially* since I received Christ in 1986. Somehow the notion that brokenness would give me a closer walk with God was foreign to my thinking.

In 1990, after seventeen years of marriage and no children, Jerry and I felt prompted by the Lord one Saturday night to pray that we would conceive a child. We had given up years earlier and resigned ourselves to being a family of just the two of us. But that evening we were lead to pray Hannah's prayer (1 Sam. 1:1–20), and felt that if we ever had a son, we were to name him Samuel—"because I asked the Lord for him" (v. 20). I remember telling Jerry, "If God gave me a child, I would know he really loved me." That night we conceived our only child, due on Christmas. The doctor did an ultrasound at seven and a half weeks and reassured me that my baby was healthy. I couldn't believe what I saw on the screen! Our little baby looked like Charlie Brown, with tiny arms and legs and a precious little heart that beat with a red bleep on the screen.

Five weeks later I was in the emergency room, miscarrying the only child I would ever have.

You know what? I haven't always done brokenness the "right" way. Being broken and at the feet of Jesus is quite different than being broken and angry, broken and bitter, broken and unchanged, broken and rebellious, broken and alone. I've done it all those ways—but God still didn't let me go.

The words I spoke on the night I conceived our baby—that if God would give me a child, I would know he really loved me—got retranslated into "God doesn't really love me." One year after my miscarriage, I started my journey back to the cross to rediscover the God I loved as a little girl, when I believed God was all good.

As a little Catholic girl, I read every book on the saints I could find. Their lives were lives of brokenness, not prosperity (at least not by the world's standards). They were doers of faith, but more importantly, they were *be*-ers of faith, abiding in the vine and being pruned—not only of unproductive branches but also of productive ones. The pruning prepared them to produce even more fruit, and the sacrifice of their broken hearts furnished a pleasing fragrance to the Lord.

Does the Lord ask any less of us as his saints?

When we face brokenness, we have choices. We may choose to move *around* the brokenness and not face the pain. Or we may choose to *dwell* on the pain and never choose to go through it. Or we may choose to *surrender* and be like the little child who says, "Daddy, pick me up. Carry me. Hold me. I can't, but you can." We can choose to offer the sacrifice of a broken and contrite heart and let God use it. That choice is a journey toward God—not for *our* healing but *for his glory*.

Does that mean God didn't care about my healing from the loss of my child? That my pain was insignificant in the sight of an awesome God who has more important things to do? No. But God is more interested in being with me through the suffering than in ending the pain. Does God see the loss of my only baby as good, so he can teach me higher things? Again, no. Of all people, he knows what it was like to sacrifice his only Son. But he used my pain and transformed it.

I'm not sure when it happened, but somewhere along the way things changed. God made me more compassionate. He taught me about grief and loss. He taught me the power of weeping with those who weep. He taught me not to rescue people from their pain but to be with them in it. He taught me to forgive those who hurt me with inappropriate words.

I wish I could have just read a few good books on grief rather than experience the pain firsthand, but the results wouldn't have been the same.

In counseling, our ultimate goal is not for the counselees to be healed of their presenting problem; it is that working through their brokenness will lead them closer to God. The violations to our clients' beings through abuse, neglect, and love deprivation create a breach in our relationship with Father God. Jerry and I are called to be repairers of the breach and restorers of homes to dwell in (Isa. 58:12). Homes for *God* to dwell in; homes where worship, trust, obedience, repentance, and brokenness are permanent fixtures.

C. S. Lewis said, "When I invited Jesus into my life, I thought He was going to put up some wallpaper and hang a few pictures. But He started knocking out walls and adding on rooms. I said, 'I was expecting a nice cottage.' But He said, 'I'm making a palace in which to live.'"[9]

God is calling us to a journey of brokenness which in this life is never ending. It is a daily walk. It's not only about life and living but also about death and dying. It's not about doing but being; not about performing but abiding.

It's not about us. It's about him.

And that makes our journey of brokenness worth it all.

PRAYER

Oh, God, I am so fragile. My dreams get broken, my relationships get broken, my heart gets broken, my body gets broken. What can I believe except that you will not despise a broken heart; that old and broken people shall yet dream dreams; and that the lame shall leap for joy, the blind see, and the deaf hear. What can I believe, except what Jesus taught—that only what is first broken, like bread, can be shared; that only what is broken is open to your entry; that old wineskins must be ripped open and replaced if the wine of new life is to expand.[10]

THOUGHTS AND REFLECTIONS

Engaging my brokenness will enlarge my heart and increase my capacity to love.

AND DARKNESS IS MY CLOSEST FRIEND

I believe in the sun even when it isn't shining.
I believe in love even when I don't feel it.
I believe in God even when He is silent.
—*Auschwitz Holocaust Victim*

In 2002, Jerry and I took a two-week journey to Israel with a personal guide who traveled with us. It was during the Intifada, which meant few tourists. We could stay at different sites as long as we wanted without having to share the moments with others.

One day in Jerusalem, we journeyed from the garden of Gethsemane down the very steps Jesus walked to face Pilate. Passing small caverns under the temple where prisoners were scourged, we descended a series of narrow steps deeper and deeper underground. At the bottom was a podium, and on the podium sat a notebook containing Psalm 88 written in every language known to man.

I was taken aback. Psalm 88 was *my* psalm. I never considered that it was Jesus's psalm first before he shared it with me.

It had been a very dark season for me, one in which the rug had been pulled out from under me time and time again. Whenever I had a little piece of hope, it would be dashed. What started as a shallow grave had me ten stories down, not even wanting to try to get up again.

The truth is, sometimes life doesn't get better. It gets worse. It gets lonelier. More painful. There are more tears—or none at all. Just numbness. Anger. Spewing. Silence. Emptiness. Lots of "Whys?" but no answers.

Have you noticed that Psalm 88 ends differently from any other psalm? There is no concluding verse that brings encouragement and hope. There is a dead end stop before any of that happens: "and darkness is my closest friend"—period. That's it, end of story. Yet somehow that verse encouraged me during my darkest night. God left the end of that psalm open and made room for desperate times of sorrow and pain. Psalm 88 offered me empathy, that someone could just sit with me in my pain and love me.

My loving Father has met, and will yet meet me, here—in the grave, the pit, the closet, the darkness. Is it not the Lord who allures us into the wilderness—into the Valley of Achor (which means "trouble") (Hos. 2:14–15)? And during that valley experience, are there not rich and deep revelations that could never be learned without struggle and wrestling? This darkness, so fearful and full of pain, may be necessary for us to grasp a dependence on God such as we could never know apart from it.

PRAYER

Take a few minutes to prayerfully ponder Psalm 139:7–12 from The Message:

"Is there anyplace I can go to avoid your Spirit? To be out of your sight? If I climb to the sky, you're there! If I go underground, you're there! If I flew on morning's wings to the far western horizon, you'd find me in a minute— you're already there waiting! Then I said to myself, 'Oh, he even sees me in the dark! At night I'm immersed in the light!' It's a fact: darkness isn't dark to you; night and day, darkness and light, they're all the same to you."

THOUGHTS AND REFLECTIONS

God is good no matter what, even when we do not understand his ways.

AMAZING GRACE: THE TOO-GOOD-TO-BE-TRUE GOOD NEWS

I used up all my energy trying to outperform
the jerk that I know I am inside.
—*A Young Man Struggling with Self-hatred*

In our profession, the issue of grace comes up over and over. It has become overwhelmingly obvious to us that many true, God-loving believers either do not understand the true meaning of grace or else they have personally disqualified themselves from receiving it. Either way, they fail to experience the reality of the gospel—the too-good-to-be-true good news that came when Jesus arrived in our lives.

As believers in Christ, we are not defined by our sin or our struggle. Yes, we struggle and we sin, but our core identity—who we really are—has been transformed. *We are not sinners who have been forgiven (as important as God's forgiveness is) but lovers of God who have a good and redeemed nature.* If our true identity has been redeemed, then our heart is not sinful but righteous. Our heart is good.

If we do not internalize this truth, we will always focus on getting better and sinning less instead of resting in the love of Father God and allowing his kindness to lead us toward change (Rom. 2:4).

Grace is God's antidote for shame. We are accepted by him with no possibility of rejection. Accepted once and accepted forever at the ultimate core of our being. This is the too-good-to-be-true good news of grace.

PRAYER FOR THE JOURNEY

As we begin Week Nine, we open our hearts to your precious gift of grace and pray:

Father, I am grateful for the work of Jesus in my life. Although I was once lost in my sinful nature, yet because of my faith in you, I am now your beloved child and a new creation. Yet I still struggle to grasp this reality. I struggle with believing that you see me as righteous and with seeing myself in that truth.

Father, when I reject this truth in the deepest place, I reject the completed work of your Son. I don't want that. Lord, I declare that when you look upon me, you see me as your righteous child. Therefore, I too declare that I am righteous—a saint, a holy one set apart by you and for you.

Lord, I want to fulfill the destiny and calling that you have placed within me. I want to fly, not crawl. I want to be transformed into more of your likeness and into the fullness of whom you created me to be. But Lord, I know I cannot do this on my own. I submit my heart to you, and I invite you to reveal, heal, and lead me in this transforming work. I choose to trust you, for you are a good Father who desires the best for me. Please continue to take these truths into the deepest places of my heart, and give me the grace—your enabling power—to see, love, and accept myself, and then others, the way you do.

MAKE ME WEAK

*I'd rather be disliked for who I am than to be
admired for who I'm not.*
—*Cecil Murphey*

One way to get the attention of our clients—especially our male clients—
is to tell them we are going to pray and ask God to make them weak. You
may be thinking the same thing our clients think: "Why in the world
would I want to pray that?" The answer is, becoming weak is the only way
to have true strength. Let us explain.

As we walk through this life, and the many difficult things that come
our way, we develop ways to deal with things. Ways to survive. We learn
how to become strong, self-sufficient, self-reliant—but that strength is
rooted in our own flesh, not in the power of God living within us. This
can be especially true in those who have not had enough love and nurture
while growing up, and in those who were emotionally, spiritually, physically, or sexually abused.

Often, when a person has learned to function out of self-reliance, that
man or woman seems to need little help from others—including God.
The person may say otherwise, but the way he or she lives and inter-
acts in relationships does not support their words. In fact, people living
from this place often have a difficult time even identifying that they have
needs. Also, those who have "survived" for a long time prior to becoming
a Christian may not have truly made the transfer of power that is funda-
mental to the Christian faith.

Although the world—and even the Western church—applauds the strong, self-sufficient individual, such a person may actually be functioning in opposition to God and his will. Their independence can be a form of pride: not the overtly arrogant pride that we identify quite easily but the kind that says, "I can handle it myself; I can make it; I don't need anyone else's help, including God's."

Many people have a strong aversion to weakness, whether their own or someone else's. Unfortunately, we often have a distorted concept of what healthy, biblical weakness means. What does it look like according to God's definition? One of the most important Scriptures, which God has emphasized for us over and over, is what Paul wrote in 2 Corinthians 12:9:

> [The Lord] said to me, "My grace is sufficient for you, for my power is made perfect in weakness." Therefore I will boast all the more gladly about my weaknesses, so that Christ's power may rest on me.

Christ spoke this to Paul at a time when the apostle was asking for relief from a recurring struggle of some type (Paul called it a "thorn"). Listen to Paul as he continues in verse 10:

> For Christ's sake, I delight in weaknesses, in insults, in hardships, in persecutions, in difficulties. For when I am weak, then I am strong.

Few would call Paul a weakling in his Christian life, yet he invited and embraced weakness so that the fullness of God's power could be at work in him. He knew he could not make it on his own power. He could not fulfill the call on his life with anything less than the true power of God—God's *dunamis* (the Greek word from which our English word *dynamite* derives). He knew he had to surrender. Paul embraced godly weakness. Will you?

PRAYER

Father, I need to experience your strength at work in me. Please make me weak so I can live depending on your strength, not my own. I choose to trust you with this—with me.

THOUGHTS AND REFLECTIONS

Father God, I surrender. Make me weak so you can be strong.

YOU'RE MY EVERYTHING

God in my hoping, there in my dreaming
God in my watching, God in my waiting
God in my laughing, there in my weeping
God in my hurting, God in my healing
Be my everything, be my everything
—Tim Hughes, "Everything"
Used by permission

On his album *Level Ground*, Brian Doerksen shares this truth: "No matter what we've done, we are all on level ground because of grace."[11] On his DVD of the same title, Brian interviews people who have fallen hard from grace—murderers, drug dealers, thieves, people Brian met in his prison ministry who have discovered that, because of Christ and the grace he extends, they are restorable, redeemable, and loveable. Grace extends to each of us because the price is paid by Jesus Christ for every sin ever committed.

I (Denise) was listening to Brian's rendition of the Tim Hughes song "Everything," enjoying its cadence and rhythm, when it struck me that something was missing. Certainly it's good news to know that God is in my working, sleeping, and breathing. But I need to know he is also with me when I'm screwing up, whether a little or a lot, even amid costly choices and life-altering mistakes.

During a counseling session with one couple, Jerry and I were stressing how Emmanuel, God with Us, could never separate from us or leave us. I told the husband that even when he is looking at pornography, God is right there with him, with his arm around him—that nothing could ever separate him from God's presence. *Nothing.* The husband stared at me for a fraction of a second and then said, "I wish he would step out of the room for that."

Thankfully, God can't take him up on his request. The definition of *never* is "not ever"; *nothing* means "not a single thing"; and *always* means "all ways." No exceptions.

Here are the lyrics to "Everything" by Tim Hughes.

Everything (God in My Living)

God in my living, there in my breathing
God in my waking, God in my sleeping
God in my resting, there in my working
God in my thinking, God in my speaking
Be my everything, be my everything
God in my hoping, there in my dreaming
God in my watching, God in my waiting
God in my laughing, there in my weeping
God in my hurting, God in my healing
Be my everything, be my everything

Christ in me, the hope of glory
You are everything
(Used by permission)

As counselors, we envision lyrics of our own, inspired by Hughes's powerful song, that speak to the gritty issues people deal with.

God when I'm lusting, there when I'm cheating
God when I'm lying, God when I'm stealing
God when I'm raging, there when I'm screaming
God when I'm judging, God when I'm blaming
You are there with me, you are there with me

God when I'm hiding, there when I'm faking
God when I'm shaming, God when I'm hating
When I'm betraying, there when I'm failing
God when I'm pleading, God when I'm begging
You are here with me, Jesus, here with me

God when I'm cursing, when I'm abusing
There when I'm drugging, when I'm self-loathing
God when I'm damning, when I'm defiling
God in my darkness, there you are waiting

You're right here with me, Jesus, here with me
Father here with me, always here with me

PRAYER

Father, you say in your Word that nothing can separate us from your love and that you will never leave us or forsake us. Your Word never lies. But it is shocking: a holy God who never leaves us. Your grace—this too-good-to-be-true good news—is scandalous, staggering.

Is there any other word to describe the God and Creator of all things who would come as a man to save his creation? Father, thank you that I mean that much to you that you will never leave me. You are always right next to me, with your arm around me. I can rest in that. I can rest in you.

THOUGHTS AND REFLECTIONS

Grace does not depend on anything we can do to earn it nor anything we could do to lose it. It is a free, universal, spontaneous gift.

THE STORY OF GRACE

This vulgar grace is indiscriminate compassion. It works
without asking anything of us. It's not cheap. It's free, and as
such will always be a banana peel for the orthodox foot and
a fairy tale for the grown-up sensibility. Grace is sufficient
even though we huff and puff with all our might to try to find
something or someone it cannot cover. Grace is enough.
He is enough. Jesus is enough.
—Brennan Manning

I (Denise) was prompted recently by a close friend to write the story of Grace. It is not the story of God's grace, but of the little black-and-white bundle of a border collie that showed up on our doorstep twelve years ago.

Jerry and I were not looking for an addition to our family of "just the two of us." Losing our Sheltie the previous year had torn our hearts out. After my miscarriage in 1990, Lassie had brought life into our home. Losing her as suddenly as we lost our baby twelve years prior rocked our world. While Jerry had been unable to grieve the loss of our child at the time, the loss of Lassie removed all hindrances for him to grieve. Describing this time in our lives, Jerry says, "We hit the wall." We stopped doing life and ministry and took a break from our counseling practice. We were already tired and burned out, and Lassie's death was the final straw.

So we were not so ready to receive a "gift package" in a crate. We were just returning home from a weekend of personal ministry in West Virginia, and it had been a good trip. We pulled into our driveway at dusk, and I could see something in the driveway. I pointed it out to Jerry, and as we got closer, I said, "Oh my gosh, it's a crate and there is a puppy in it!" As I got out of the car, I also saw a bag of dog food, a sack of toys, and a letter:

Hello!

I am a miracle dog in need of someone to love who will love me in return. I am a border collie who is almost five months old. I was born on a farm to two working border collies. They worked hard herding but were very happy. They had a stall of their very own in the barn, and they were really excited that me and my brothers and sister were coming soon. Their owner was a nice lady who was very old and who got very sick. No one knew how sick she was for a long time, so my mommy and daddy didn't eat for two whole weeks.

My daddy got really hungry and sick, and he died before we were born. My mommy was sick too, but she knew she had to stay around to have us four puppies. When we were born, only me and my little brother were alive, and he was very sick too. Finally, someone came and found us, but it ended up being too late for my brother. He died in a hospital. Mommy was really mad that no one came sooner and didn't want anyone to touch her. She growled and bit a lot, and then she had to go away too. That made me sad, but now she is with Daddy and the other puppies, so she is happy! I am the only member of my family left, but I know that is no accident! For some reason, God had other plans for me.

Thanks for finding a place in your heart for me. I will be your life-long companion, and I thank God for allowing me to live and for giving you to me. He is such an awesome God!

Jerry and I were actually quite upset. Who would just drop a dog on someone's doorstep with all the fixings included? What if we did not want or weren't ready for another responsibility? We had just started traveling more for ministry and on mission outreaches outside the country, and this would definitely complicate things.

The poor little puppy was so scared, she just found a corner of a rug downstairs and laid down. I told her, "You can stay in my house, but you are not getting into my heart." But the next morning when we came downstairs, do you know where I found her? Right in my heart.

We knew immediately that her name was Grace because . . .

In West Virginia, driving through the countryside, Jerry asked God to let him see some deer, and he counted fifteen that day.

We arrived home on September 15.

Our flight number was 555.

In biblical numerology, five is the number of grace. So, grace, grace, grace three times. And then a surprise gift on our doorstep. All in the same day.

We called everyone we knew to find out who did it. No one admitted anything. We didn't have a clue.

No doubt you've heard the question, "What's in a name?" Grace had no difficulty owning hers. Our veterinarian was deeply moved when he met Grace and heard her story; he even made a copy of the letter she came with. Several of the clients we see in our home ask for her specifically; she gives them a sense of safety and protection. Grace is sensitive to their tears and will come close to them when she senses they are hurting.

One client, sitting cross-legged on the floor as he shared some of his painful past, broke down crying. Grace was instantly there with him, face to face, to comfort him. She was just what he needed. Amazed at her sensitivity toward him, the man felt in that moment that she represented the Father's love and affection toward him. Grace actually received an evaluation from him and got—what else?—five out of five.

Last fall, eleven years after Grace showed up at our home and in our hearts, we received a call from a good friend whom we had not seen in a long time. We could not figure out why she was so upset. She said the Lord had convicted her to finally be honest with us: she was the one who had left Grace in our driveway. Would we forgive her?

That had to be the easiest forgiveness we have ever extended to anyone!

You know, it is nice to know that final part of the story, but it really doesn't change anything. . . .

Grace has always been a too-good-to-be-true gift in our lives. We did nothing to earn it. We walk with Grace and thank God for Grace. There is nothing quite like Grace. God made a home for Grace in our hearts. Thank you, Father, for the ongoing miracle of Grace in our lives.

(And by the way, God, thank you too for our border collie, Grace.)

PRAYER

Father, I want to tell you a zillion times and never be tired of it—thank you, thank you, thank you for your gift of grace for me. Absolutely incredible.

THOUGHTS AND REFLECTIONS

Because of the gift of grace, I am free to become, and to come to be, all that God created me to be.

REMEMBER RAHAB

Love is to reveal the beauty of another person to themselves.
—*Jean Vanier*

A woman in her late twenties came to our ministry for a few days of intensive counseling. She was distraught over knowing God loved her but not being able to experience or sense his love for her personally. Was she doing something wrong? Had he forgiven her for her sordid past?

The woman had grown up in a sexually perverted family. As a little girl, she was exposed to all kinds of pornography and lewd behavior. It was the perfect setup for the enemy. The abuse began when she was twelve, with her father selling her "services" to a married friend. She felt dirty and ashamed. She wondered what she had done to deserve something like that.

That incident was the first in a recurring pattern—partly through her father's soliciting men and partly through relationships she herself pursued. She was always looking for someone to love her. At seventeen she had a daughter out of wedlock, and her brother started sexually abusing the little girl before she was five. The generational sin kept on drawing the children into its web. The horror stories the woman shared with us went on and on.

One night, while she was crying about her shame and worthlessness, a neighbor woman knocked on the door and invited her to church. This was her divine appointment, orchestrated by a loving God. She was introduced to Jesus and turned her life around.

But, she told us, "I have felt like a prostitute all my life and have even called myself one. I asked for forgiveness, but I never felt clean enough for God." She continued, "I'm afraid God is going to turn away from me and say he never knew me—that his promises are too good to be true for someone like me."

On our final day of counseling, we moved into a time of healing prayer, listening to the Lord for his direction. Just as Jerry was praying about the cross of Christ, she excitedly interrupted: "God showed me a picture of the cross right before Jerry started praying it. Then I heard God's tender voice speak just two words to me: 'Remember Rahab.'"

The woman began to weep and laugh at the same time. She had heard God's voice loud and clear. God saw her and knew her. But what he said to her left her speechless. Those two words, "Remember Rahab," were profound and meaningful to her. It was a moment in God Jerry and I could never have orchestrated.

Interestingly, I had just finished a novel about Rahab, so our client's words were especially impactful. Let's look again at Rahab's story, found in Joshua chapters 2 and 6.

Around 1,400 years before Christ, Joshua was chosen by God to succeed Moses and lead Israel into Canaan, the Promised Land. Joshua and his armies were sent into the cities of Canaan and were instructed by God to totally destroy every king and every breathing thing. Joshua sent two men to spy on Jericho. When they arrived at the walled city, they came to a public house, where Rahab the harlot lived, to stay for the night.

Word quickly traveled to the king, and the king's men came to Rahab's door, demanding the spies. But Rahab had hidden the men under some stalks of flax that were drying on her roof. "They've left," she told the soldiers. She hadn't realized who they were, she said, and she didn't know where they were headed. "Go quickly," she said. "You might still catch them."

When the soldiers were gone, Rahab went back up to the men on her roof. She knew their God was the one true God, she said, and she begged the men to spare her and her household. The men agreed, and at the time appointed by God, when Joshua and his army conquered Jericho, Rahab and her family were the only inhabitants whose lives were spared. They lived in the Promised Land with the Israelites from that day on.

Now here is the astounding part: Fourteen hundred years later, Matthew rolled out the lineage of Christ in the first chapter of his gospel. It is here, in verse 5, that we actually find out what happened to Rahab: "Salmon the father of Boaz, whose mother was Rahab . . ." So Salmon—a leader with Joshua from the lineage of Abraham—married a non-Israelite woman with a sordid past (unheard of on both counts), and they had a son, Boaz. The lineage continues through King David and ends with the birth of Jesus. A prostitute is found in the family tree of Christ! Her faith is celebrated among the greats in Hebrews 11:31, and her righteousness is likened to Abraham's in James 2:25. Absolutely amazing.

"Remember Rahab." Two small words that set a young woman free.

Thank you, Father, that you don't look at the sin—you look at the heart.

PRAYER

Father, thank you that I have been grafted into the lineage of Jesus—just like Rahab. Thank you for saving me from death and adopting me as your own—just like Rahab. Father, as with Rahab, you planned from the beginning of time to share your heart and incredible love with me. I have tried to be good enough, clean enough, "fine" enough, but I can't, any more than Rahab could. Under the law of the land, she would have been judged as a prostitute and a pagan and been killed. But Father, you saw Rahab's heart and you rescued her.

Thank you for your Son, who set me free from the law and gave me the freedom to run right into your throne of grace. I too need to be reminded to "remember Rahab." You looked at her heart and saw faith. Create that kind of faith in me, Father, and continue to grow me up as your child. I welcome you to take my breath away with your poignant, unfathomable love.

THOUGHTS AND REFLECTIONS

The bottom line is this: As a believer in Christ, I am not defined by my sin or my struggle. My heart is good.

I AM STILL RIGHTEOUS

What is in our "heart" matters more than anything
else for who we become.
—Dallas Willard

Does the chapter title make you pause? "*Still* righteous? Have I ever thought I was righteous in the first place?" Making such a claim sounds pretty arrogant, doesn't it. Let's take that a step further: *I have a good heart.* How does that sound? Still a bit prideful?

When people hear the words, "You have a good heart" or "You are righteous," an internal resistance often rises up. What typically follows (though not necessarily verbalized) is something like "You don't know what I've been struggling with," or "You don't know what I just said to my spouse," or a multitude of other you-don't-knows.

Guess what: It doesn't matter. You are still righteous.

We don't mean that your thoughts and behaviors don't matter. After all, we are called to walk in love toward God, self, and others, and it is God's desire that our lives demonstrate the fruit of the Spirit (Gal. 5:22–23). But do my thoughts and behaviors determine the condition of my heart? No. They don't change it from good to bad.

But wait. Doesn't it say in Jeremiah 17:9 that the heart is "deceitfully wicked above all things" (our rendering)? Yes it does. But something— actually someone—changed this: Jesus Christ.

When you placed your trust in Jesus Christ and invited him into your heart, you were changed, and the true nature of your heart was changed as well.

"But if this is true, why do I continue to sin?" We'll go after that in a bit. Right now, let's unpack this "scandalous" belief about a good heart with a look at what the Scriptures say about it.

The New Testament uses the word *saint* to identify a follower of Jesus Christ. It comes from the Greek word *hagios*, which means "holy." Scripture is clear concerning the nature of those who have given their hearts to Christ. Our identity is no longer based on our "old nature"; we have been given a *new* nature, and *it* is who we really are.

> Therefore, if anyone is in Christ, he is a new creation; the old has gone, the new has come! (2 Cor. 5:17 NIV 1984)

> For we know that our old self was crucified with him [Christ] so that the body of sin might be done away with, that we should no longer be slaves to sin—because anyone who has died has been freed from sin. (Rom. 6:6–7 NIV 1984)

Again, as believers in Christ, we are not the same as before. Our old nature has died, and Jesus now lives in and through us: "For you died, and your life is now hidden with Christ in God" (Col. 3:3). Our core identity is now righteous, no matter what we do or do not do. This true identity is not based in ourselves but in what Christ has accomplished through his death and resurrection and by our placing our faith in him (Rom. 4:24; Phil. 3:9).

So why do I still struggle if I have a good and redeemed heart and my true nature is as a righteous saint? Countless Christians have struggled with this question over the years; they have felt anything but righteous. For many, the very process of seeking counseling actually seems to contradict this truth. They think things like

> *If there wasn't something inherently wrong with me, I wouldn't need counseling in the first place.*

If I were "righteous," then I wouldn't have this problem with (anger/ addiction/fear/___).

If I were "righteous," I wouldn't keep doing the same thing over and over and keep hurting my wife/my children/myself.

Mark the following point. It's so important! *Although we have become new people spiritually, we still live in a body that harbors the remnants of sin.* We still live in a world where the "flesh" (our old nature) is in conflict with the Spirit of God within us (our new nature):

> For the flesh desires what is contrary to the Spirit, and the Spirit what is contrary to the flesh. They are in conflict with each other. (Gal. 5:17)

So does any of this really matter? Yes. We believe it matters a great deal. The bottom line is this: *As a believer in Christ, I am not defined by my sin or my struggle.* Yes, I struggle and I sin, but my core identity—who I *really* am—is not a sinner who has been forgiven, as important as that is, but a lover of God who has a good and redeemed nature. And if my true identity has been redeemed, then my heart (spirit) is not sinful but righteous—it is good.

If I do not internalize this truth, I will always be focusing on "getting better" and sinning less instead of resting in the love of Father God and allowing his kindness to lead me to repentance (change) (Rom. 2:4).

As we continue on this journey of sanctification, or healing, which includes identifying our core areas of wounding and our sinful responses to those wounds, we must never lose sight of how the Father sees us or how he feels toward us.

Remember, he is the God who runs to embrace sinners—including those who live in his house (see Luke 15:11–32). Through the work of his Son, he does *not* see us as sinners, but as his righteous saints. And if that is how he sees us, should we not see ourselves the same way?

PRAYER

Father, I am grateful for the work of Jesus in my life. Although I was once lost in my sinful nature, now, because of my faith in your Son, I am your beloved child and a new creation. Thank you for adopting me into your family. Thank you that I have the spirit of sonship and am not an orphan. I still struggle with these truths. I still struggle with believing that you see me as righteous, and I struggle with seeing myself in that truth. I want to be able to rest securely in this identity.

I declare that when you look upon me, you see me as your righteous child, and therefore I too declare that I am righteous. A saint. A holy one set apart by you and for you. Please continue to take this truth into the deepest place in my heart.

THOUGHTS AND REFLECTIONS

_____

_____

_____

_____

_____

_____

_____

_____

_____

_____

_____

_____

_____

_____

_____

_____

_____

_____

_____

_____

_____

_____

_____

_____

_____

_____

_____

God doesn't stop at merely saving us from judgment; he changes us into something we were not before. That is exactly the awesome miracle that occurs when we become new creatures in Christ!

BE GOOD TO YOU +
BE GOD TO YOU =
LOVING WHO GOD LOVES

Your life and my life are, each of them, one of a kind.
No one has lived your life or my life before, and no one will
ever live them again. Our lives are unique stones in the mosaic
of human existence—priceless and irreplaceable.
—Henri Nouwen

We have now come full circle back to the premise of this book: loving God and loving myself. We must love God with all our heart and love ourselves, and like ourselves, just as much as God loves us and really likes us. Then we must turn around and love others the same way.

When we can truly trust the loving heart of the Father toward us, then we can begin to love ourselves as he does by being gentle, grace-filled, responsible, caring, and attentive to ourselves. In this way, we can discover who God says we are and grow in that direction. From this place of identity, the Father will unveil our destiny, the plans he has for us. We will then be free to be all he created us to be.

PRAYER FOR THE JOURNEY

As we conclude these final steps of our journey in Week Eleven, pray with us for the Father's loving guidance:

Father, thank you for your process of redemption and restoration—big words that have a simple meaning: I am important enough to you that you made a way to find me, heal my heart, and bring me to a new place. Thank you that you sent your Son, Jesus, to heal my broken heart and set me free from the things I know I am unable to do without your help, including living from a place of freedom and life. Please help me continue to love and accept myself and live from your heart. Help me love you, myself, and others the way you intend.

LOVING GOD, SHOW ME THE TRUTH ABOUT MYSELF

Loving God,
show me the truth about myself,
no matter how wonderful it may be.
—Cecil Murphey

Let's read the above quote again, and this time make it a prayer:

Loving God,

show me the truth about myself,

no matter how wonderful it may be. [12]

Does that last line grip your heart like it does mine? I can feel my heart smiling—especially since I am expecting a whammy. The end of that prayer takes me pleasantly off guard.

I (Denise) remember being taught the Examination of Conscience when I was seven years old, as I was preparing to confess my sins to the priest. It was a serious, soul-searching process for me, and I wanted to include everything I had done wrong or failed to do right.

We all know we are to confess our sins, struggles, and failures to God and receive his forgiveness and mercy in return. But what if one of our greatest struggles—the struggle that hurts God profoundly—is failing to love what he loves: us? What if our lack of love for ourselves cuts his heart deeply? What if he longs for us to forgive the self we are so hard on, hold in contempt, and refuse to love or accept?

Why are we looking for God to find something wrong with us, as if he is never pleased with us? Is it because we are afraid that maybe we don't pray enough, love enough, serve enough, or give enough? Or perhaps are critical, selfish, or a poser?

What if he just delights in us—rough edges and all? What if he enjoys what he created in us . . . desires to encourage us on the journey . . . and wants us to know that his heart overflows with love, acceptance, and affirmation of who he has created us to be?

He already knows we will make mistakes—and he knows we can learn from our failures and disappointments and struggles. He isn't waiting for us to "arrive" at some top pinnacle on this earth. He just wants to be right with us as we grow—needing him, being dependent on him, and leaning on him along the way.

Would you consider stopping at different moments today to ask God what wonderful truths he sees when he looks at you? Maybe it could become part of your daily diet—like an essential nutrient. Because it really is.

PRAYER

Loving God, show me the truth about myself, no matter how wonderful it may be.

THOUGHTS AND REFLECTIONS

_____

_____

_____

_____

_____

_____

_____

_____

_____

_____

_____

_____

_____

_____

_____

_____

_____

_____

_____

_____

_____

_____

_____

_____

_____

*Repeat this verse throughout the day (throughout your whole life, actually):
"I am the one Jesus loves." It has a nice ring to it, doesn't it? What a wonderful change it would be from your usual self-talk.*

AHA-MOMENTS WITH GOD

If we take all the goodness, wisdom, and compassion
of the best mothers and fathers who have ever lived,
they would only be a faint shadow of the love and mercy
in the heart of the redeeming God.
—*Brennan Manning*

We all know God is everywhere, and he can't be any closer to us than he already is, has been, and always will be. So, contrary to some church signs you've seen, no one can ever actually move away from him, nor he from us. Yet there are times when Abba Father reveals that he is right there with us—closer than our breath. Jerry and I call these surprises "aha-moments" with him. Let us share some of those aha-stories to help build your faith in Father God's nature.

God has shown up in cars in the middle of rush-hour traffic. One man pulled to the side of the road and wept and wept in God's healing presence. He called us from his car and asked why God did not show up in his prayer time that morning when it was convenient. It is just like God to show up when we are not in control!

For one woman, God showed up in the shower, personally washing away her sense of stain and filth from sexual defilement by her father. We thought this was a pretty bold move on God's part. When she called me right after this experience, all I could think was "Yikes." How much more counseling was she going to need after this? But of course God was very gentle with her. Minutes later, she was naked and unashamed—an aha-moment times a thousand.

God has shown up in the middle of a business man's presentation. Tears welled up in the man's eyes—a special touch from of his Abba Father, who wanted his son to know he was proud of him.

Father God has made appearances in closets, under the bed, in toy boxes, in pup tents, and in the sandbox, making roads for a little boy's hot cars. God has shown up on dirt roads, elevators, airplanes, and beaches to meet with his children. One man found Father God next to him while he was sinning; he immediately stopped what he was doing.

A strong woman of faith told us her story of a time years back when she had fallen away from the Lord. Coming home to her apartment one evening, she discovered, written in the dust on her bedside table, her favorite Scripture which had been spoken over her when she received salvation. She was in awe: "He knows me and sees me." She dropped down to her knees and rededicated her life to Christ. She has been a missionary ever since.

Once, while traveling the hill country of Texas, Jerry and I stopped at a park to take a break. Jerry took out his guitar and we sat on top of a table, singing worship songs together. Three longhorn cattle came to the fence and listened to us. That was pretty cool. I told Jerry that the longhorns were fine, but I really wanted to see a lamb. Just then there was a commotion to the side of us, and—you guessed right—a lamb was running right toward us, with a man in hot pursuit. The man told us the lamb had broken through the fence and got away. We thought, "Of course he got away. God wanted us to see a lamb." What an intimate, loving Father, who cares about every detail!

All such moments, whether our own or those that others have shared with us, give us a glimpse into the Father's heart. And what child cannot love a Father who loves like that!

PRAYER

Dear Father God,

I know that all I am is already found in you; I am made in your image. Remind me again how you see me when I am feeling less than worthy of love. Remind me again that you will never leave me orphaned—rejected, alone, or abandoned. Lord, remind me that the most destructive wound of abandonment is when I orphan myself. Forgive me for not loving myself and not seeing myself reflected in your eyes.

I love that you love me, even when I'm being unlovable. What a great deal that is for me. I want to extend to myself the same amount of grace you offer me. Remove my walls of defense and self-protection. Dismantle my fortifications that protect me from pain, fear, and shame. I invite you to meet me at my most vulnerable times—times that may not be convenient by the world's standards but that are perfect for you. I look forward to an aha-moment with you. I'll be waiting.

Your Child

THOUGHTS AND REFLECTIONS

_____

_____

_____

_____

_____

_____

_____

_____

_____

_____

_____

_____

_____

_____

_____

_____

_____

_____

_____

_____

_____

_____

_____

_____

_____

_____

_____

_____

_____

_____

If I don't measure up enough for me, I will never be able to internalize and believe the love and care that God and others have for me.

TURTLE TRACKS

*Turtle Tracks. It is not an ice cream flavor. It is not a
chocolate, pecan, and caramel candy. It is not a flavored coffee.
It's a journey from the nest to the sea. It's destiny.*
—Denise Basel

One of our favorite island destinations in Florida is also a prolific breeding ground for loggerhead sea turtles. We seldom see one of these turtles, but the nests where they lay their eggs are clearly marked along the twenty-two-mile beach. The rules are strict: It's "lights out" for the homes along the beachfront. Curtains drawn. Blinds closed. Porch lights off.

You see, the eggs usually hatch at night, when there is less danger that the baby turtles will be eaten by predators. Once they pop out of the nest, they make a run to the sea—unless they become distracted and taken off course by bright lights. If that happens, they may never make it to where they are meant to go.

Sitting on the beach alone one afternoon, I saw movement out of the corner of my eye. I thought it was just another crab throwing sand as it burrowed out of its hole. It wasn't; it was a lone baby sea turtle. Jerry walked out on the deck just then, and I motioned for him to grab his camera. Quick! The little turtle was trucking really fast to get to the water. (Yes, turtles can actually go fast!) I knew Jerry would never get back soon enough to get a picture.

But then the unexpected happened. A wave came and threw the little sea turtle back up on the beach, right on its back. It was helpless to change its situation. It madly kicked its little legs, trying to flip over.

With this bit of luck (for us, not the turtle), Jerry was able to get there in time to capture the scene on the camera. I flipped the little guy over with a seashell, and he ran straight into the sea. We saw him floating on the crest of a wave, and then he was gone.

That memorable experience elicited a "Thanks, God!" in both of us. But there was even more to it. The baby loggerhead left behind something special: the story of its journey, told through its tracks in the sand. It reached its destiny, the sea, through a convoluted series of steps—and missteps. When it burrowed out of its nest, it was already going the wrong direction, heading for the beach houses (just like some of us who are "wrong" from the beginning). Sometimes it had to backtrack. Sometimes it went around in circles, ending up where it had been before.

This reminds me of the patterns we often see when we are counseling. It's like, "How did I end up here again? How do I get off this path? I'm stuck. I'm lost. I'm tired. Maybe Siri can recommend a new route—one without delays, construction, or accidents waiting to happen. You know—the path of least resistance, the fastest route to where I want to be."

Like the little turtle, we must first discover who we are (our identity) so we can then discover where we are meant to be (our destiny). This little guy entered the scene of life somewhat protected in the womb of the nest along with the other eggs. Somewhere along the way, he got left behind, orphaned and abandoned by the other hatchlings; he broke out of his shell after everyone else "left the nest," so to speak. He was supposed to make his dash to the sea in the cloak of night so predators would not notice him. But no parents were there to give him guidance.

Sometimes we also may feel as alone in our journey as this turtle did. We may determine to make it on our own, in our own strength, protected by the shell we have grown to avoid being hurt. We may beat ourselves up along the way for making the wrong choices, for getting lost, for being a loser. Then, just when we are almost "there," we get sideswiped by a wave that knocks us on our backside. Thwarted again.

This would seem like a good time to cry out to the Father to help us. Isn't it just like the enemy to try to take us out when destiny is in our reach!

But God . . .

But God, in the little turtle's story, sent a helper (me) to be right there to encourage, lend a hand, and help him get back on his feet, heading toward his destiny.

When we choose healing for our hearts, we must not be deterred by the journey. It is human nature to want a quick fix, a recipe for success, directions to the shortest route from here to there. But healing takes time—lots of time. It is sometimes very hard. There is grief. There is running and falling down. But there is also getting up and pressing forward. There is hope. There is God with his arm around us, our greatest encourager.

In Hannah Hurnard's classic book, *Hinds' Feet on High Places*, two unlikely companions are sent by the Lord to accompany the young girl Much-Afraid on her journey. Their names are Sorrow and Suffering. Remarkably, these same two companions are transformed into Grace and Glory when the destination is reached. Sounds like something Jerry and I have experienced.

Now we invite you to embrace your own turtle tracks. There is a destiny just on the horizon. Look up. There is a loving Father extending his hand to you. You're going to make it. Dad knows the way.

Safe travels.

PRAYER

Father, I choose to exchange my ways for your ways as I travel on the journey from identity to destiny. As much as I want to be healed and healed quickly, I am willing to surrender to your timing. I ask that you speak loudly enough for me to hear you. I want to follow your lead. I realize I will have to trust you more with myself. I will have to be vulnerable. I will have to stay in your healing presence, even when I want to run.

When I arrive at the destiny you have for me, my healing journey will be one of the most valuable and precious parts of my story. It is a story I must treasure and share vulnerably with others as an encouragement for them to stay in the battle for the joy set before them. But Father, first for me. First, healing and freedom and life for me. Only after receiving can I truly give to others out of an overflow of a healed heart.

Thank you, Father, that you never, ever stop pursuing me, believing in me, and loving me. You're a good, good Father. It's who you are.

THOUGHTS AND REFLECTIONS

On the healing journey, we learn what happened to us, we realize that it mattered, and we find out where we go next. Soon we will all be ready to tell our healing story—when the story of our past no longer controls us. When it is no longer stuffed down inside us, buried alive.

WRESTLING WITH GOD

*Those who trust God most are those whose faith permits them
to risk wrestling with God over the deepest questions of life.
Good hearts are captured in a divine wrestling match;
fearful, doubting hearts stay clear of the mat.*
—*Dan B. Allender*

As we continue on our healing journey, we can never bypass the necessary work of grief. At times, it may be intense—even very intense. Some have feared that if they started crying, they would never stop. To our knowledge, that has never happened.

Of the five stages of grief, there is one that seldom makes it into the process. We call this stage "wrestling with God." Many of us are familiar with this phrase from the story of Jacob in Genesis 32:22–32. In the story, Jacob is alone. A man, who is actually God, comes and wrestles with him through the night. By daybreak, seeing that he has not prevailed over Jacob, the man touches Jacob's hip and wrenches it out of joint. Yet still Jacob fights, clinging tenaciously to his opponent. "Let me go," the man says. But Jacob, in his pain, replies, "I will not let you go until you bless me."

Thus it is that God gives Jacob a new name, Israel, and proclaims a blessing over him because he has struggled with God and men and has prevailed. Jacob leaves the mat with a limp and later tells others, "I have seen God face to face, yet my life has not been snatched away."

A client once left our office furious with God over the struggles he was facing. The next week he had a story to share with Jerry and me. He was so mad at God when he left us, he said, that he was going to "let God have it." He drove down a private dirt road, got out of his Ram truck, and decided to duke it out with God. Yelling angrily at God, he shouted, "Bubba, get in the ring!"

Suddenly he heard a loving voice say to him, "You are the apple of my eye."

What? No bolt of lightning? No crispy critter? Okay, hit the pause button. Stop action.

This man was totally undone. He ran to his truck, climbed in, and took off for home. He immediately told his wife what had happened and asked her what in the heck that meant— "the apple of my eye." She told him it was in the Bible and looked up the verse with him. Anatomically, the "apple" is the pupil—the very center of the human eye. Metaphorically, it means "cherished favorite; cherished above all others." Wow. And this is for someone who just called God "Bubba"?

These are the kinds of stories we love because they reveal the love, tenderness, grace, and understanding in the Father's heart for every one of his children—no matter what. The Father knew this man's heart and knew he was really hurting.

Maybe when you read this you expected that God would be angry, critical, accusing, or punishing toward the man. But even if your earthly father would have reacted this way, you cannot overlay his image on your heavenly Father. The truth is, there is nothing you can ever do to diminish his love for you.

Jacob got in the ring fearful and desperate; he left it with a limp, discovering that his greatest need was trusting God. Oh, how much trusting God pleases God! Trust requires vulnerability. It requires leaning on God because we can't make it without him. It means laying our hearts open before him and wrestling with him over all the pain, shame, fear, and struggles that bind us. Like Jacob, we too will walk away from the ring with a limp—a limp of vulnerability, honesty, and dependency on him.

Maybe its time for you to schedule that match you've been putting off. I'm sure it will be a win-win.

PRAYER

Father, first of all forgive me for seeing you through the distorted lens of my wounds. Many of them are from my childhood; others, from the hurts, struggles, and disappointments in my life. I admit that I have often felt you were distant, aloof, critical, and demanding. I didn't know how to trust you enough to lean on you. But, I want that now. I'm asking you to touch me like you touched Jacob and make me weak in my own abilities. In my weakness, my limp, your dunamis power is made perfect. Your grace is sufficient for me to become honest, vulnerable, and my true self. For when I am weak, you are strong.

THOUGHTS AND REFLECTIONS

God isn't as concerned about anger itself. He is more concerned with revealing anger's underlying causes. We must invite him into a "holy" wrestling match with our pain—and our anger—so he can do what he does best: heal broken hearts.

RETURNING TO YOUR FIRST LOVE

The Spirit intends to investigate our whole life history, layer by layer, throwing out the junk and preserving the values that were appropriate to each stage of our human development. . . . Eventually, the Spirit begins to dig into the bedrock of our earliest emotional life. . . . As we progress toward the center where God is actually waiting for us, we are naturally going to feel that we are getting worse. This warns us that the spiritual journey is not a success story or a career move. It is rather a series of humiliations of the false self.
—Thomas Keating

The healing journey is most productive when we begin to yield our heart, soul, strength, and mind to a loving God. We tend to yield the most to seeking help when something or someone is not working out in our life—a crisis of some sort has raised its head and gotten our attention.

Whether Jerry and I have counseled clients hour-by-hour for a year or more, or for a two-to-five-day intensive, there is always a downward turn at some point in the journey where we have to face ourselves.

Some authors refer to this journey as a roller coaster, with many dips and curves. Do you remember being on a roller coaster during that slow climb to the very top of the track? And then that moment when the roller coaster headed straight down at a breakneck speed? Grown-ups love these rides, yet they hate discovering that the healing process is not a one-ticket ride. You probably need to think of it as more like a season pass. And God, as your loving Father, is the one stamping your ticket.

One author calls it the "crappy second day." She was working with a team of developers at Pixar for a three-day training conference. When they tested and retested their model (which continued to yield a difficult day in the middle), the designers came to an amazing conclusion: you *need* the struggle on the second day to reach your goal on the third.[13] That's also how it is on the healing journey. *You can't skip the struggle if you truly want to be free.*

We have come to the close of our stories and ponderings in *Loving God, Loving Myself.* We hope they have helped you stay the course of learning to love yourself the way God does. We share with you here a favorite poem on the journey of healing. May it be as encouraging and helpful a guide to you as it has been for us in our own healing journeys. It's called "Portrait of Progress" by Portia Nelson.

    I. I walk down the street.

        There is a deep hole in the sidewalk.

            I fall in.

            I am lost . . . I am helpless.

            It isn't my fault.

            It takes forever to find a way out.

    II. I walk down the same street.

        There is a deep hole in the sidewalk.

            I pretend I don't see it.

            I fall in again.

                I can't believe I'm in the same place,

                But, it isn't my fault.

                It still takes a long time to get out.

III. I walk down the same street.

There is a deep hole in the sidewalk.

I see it there.

I still fall in . . . it's a habit.

My eyes are open.

I see where I am.

It's my fault.

I get out immediately.

IV. I walk down the same street.

There is a deep hole in the sidewalk.

I walk around it.

V. I walk down another street.[14]

PRAYER

Father, thank you that wherever I am today on this journey, you are with me. I want to yield my whole heart to you, broken as it may be. I can gaze into your eyes and see my reflection, and having looked into your heart for me, I can see how much you love me. I want to see myself the way you see me; treat myself as you do, with kindness and respect; and then turn around and give my love to others.

Some may say that the greatest commandment can be summed up as Love God, love others, love self. But I am now seeing the order differently: Love God, love self, love others. Because without the first two, I will never accomplish the last.

THOUGHTS AND REFLECTIONS

I am free to feel my emotions, work through my emotions, and not shame my emotions. I am free to embrace change and growth within me. I am free to love myself and receive love because I have value and worth. I am free to be fully me.

CONCLUSION

You've made it. We hope this leg of your journey into the heart of a loving Father has been revealing and healing. We are never finished being made into his likeness. We are imperfect children in need of a Father who will never abandon us, shame us, or reject us. He can never give up on us—it's not in his nature.

We also hope you are closer to yourself—that you will not abandon yourself, shame yourself, or reject yourself. Just as God never gives up on you, guess what? He asks you to never give up on yourself.

We don't know where you are in your journey, but we encourage you to press on to obtain the prize. It is worth it.

Let us close with a story we were told.

Once upon a time, there was a teenage girl who loved to ice skate. She loved it so much that she helped teach the younger children how to skate. She knew that if they would just do what she told them to do—follow her rules—they would love it like she did.

But they hated ice skating, and they didn't like her.

She didn't understand why.

Then she realized she was trying to force them to enjoy it her way instead of sharing her *joy* of it.

She gave it one last shot. She started sharing her *excitement* for ice skating rather than her *rules*. She encouraged her students more and bossed them less.

And do you know what happened?

They fell in love with ice skating all on their own, because they could feel the *joy* she felt.

We believe this is what must happen in us as the Father heals our hearts and enlarges our capacity to love. It's called transformation—first for ourselves, and then for our world. It's not about the rules we are to follow. It is about the freedom God invites us to embrace.

When we can embrace who we really are and see ourselves through the Father's eyes, we will share in the great joy of loving God and loving ourselves.

SOURCES

Endnotes

1 Adapted from "Lorica of Saint Patrick," EWTN Global Catholic Network, http://www.ewtn.com/Devotionals/prayers/patrick.htm.

2 John Eldredge, *Waking the Dead: The Glory of a Heart Fully Alive* (Nashville: Nelson, 2003), 211–12.

3 Julianne Maki and Mark Maki, *Christian Adults in Recovery: A Ten Week Study Book* (Brea, CA, 1992), 91.

4 Sarah Dessen, *What Happened to Goodbye* (New York: Penguin Young Readers, 2011).

5 Judith MacNutt, *Love and Healing*, tape 8813, Christian Healing Ministries, 1990.

6 Gary Moon, *Falling for God: Saying Yes to His Extravagant Proposal* (Colorado Springs: Shaw, 2004), 77–88. For our purposes, we have used WLIE instead of WSIN.

7 Brother Lawrence, *The Practice of the Presence of God* (Springdale, PA: Whitaker House, 1982), 37–38.

8 Rob Bell, *Drops Like Stars: A Few Thoughts on Creativity and Suffering* (Grand Rapids: Zondervan, 2009) 108–9.

9 C. S. Lewis, quoted by Alan Nelson, *Broken in the Right Places: How God Tames the Soul* (Nashville: Nelson), 19.

10 Ted Loder, *Guerillas of Grace: Prayers for the Battle* (Minneapolis: Augsburg, 1981), 58.

11 Brian Doerksen, recording of "Everything (God in My Living)" by Tim Hughes, on *Level Ground* (Integrity, February 21, 2011), compact disc.

12 Cecil Murphey, *Knowing God, Knowing Myself: An Invitation to Daily*

Discovery (Ventura, CA: Regal, 2010), 234.

13 Brené Brown, *Rising Strong: The Reckoning. The Rumble. The Revolution.* (New York: Spiegel & Grau, 2015), 32.

14 Portia Nelson, "Portrait of Progress," quoted in Maki and Maki, *Christian Adults in Recovery: A Ten Week Study Book* (Brea, CA, 1992), 105.

PRAISE FOR
The Missing Commandment: Love Yourself

The Missing Commandment: Love Yourself is a must-read for every person going deeper into the intimate and personal love that our heavenly Father has for us. To love ourselves in a healthy way is simply coming into agreement with how God already loves us. Jerry and Denise have done an amazing job of communicating this simple yet profound truth.

—Barry Adams, Father Heart Communications;
speaker; author, *Father's Love Letter*

I have known Jerry and Denise for the better part of three decades. These two academics-turned-well-trained-counselors know suffering hearts and the heart of God like few others. In *The Missing Commandment: Love Yourself,* they place emotional and spiritual health on a solid foundation of love—for God, for others, and for self.

—Gary W. Moon, MDiv, PhD,
executive director, Dallas Willard Center for Christian
Spiritual Formation; author, *Apprenticeship with Jesus, Falling for God*

Jerry and Denise Basel are living out in a profound way what a growing movement of authors, songwriters, theologians, and everyday people have been daring to express, believe, and try on. It is the Original Good News, aimed at the lies we've been telling ourselves about us. The Basels display with winsome confidence the astonishing love of the Father; which alone allows us to love ourselves honestly, deeply and wonderfully.

—John Lynch, Bruce McNicol, and Bill Thrall,
bestselling coauthors, *The Cure, Bo's Cafe,* and *The Ascent*

When you read *The Missing Commandment: Love Yourself,* you need to be ready for open-heart surgery. As I read it, I felt the invisible hands of grace soothe the pain and numbness out of my heart. If you want to live from the whole of your heart and feel Jesus living through and in you, then this book is a must.

—Pablo Giacopelli,
professional tennis coach on the WTA Tour;
author, *Holding On Loosely* and *The Modern Fig Leaf*

I am so excited about this book that words fail me. I don't think I've read anything like it: personal and didactic at the same time in a very easy flow. I felt like I was sitting in the counseling room talking to Jerry and Denise. Their easy style of talking yet getting to the heart of the matter came through so well. I thought of my clients in the addiction center and knew just how much I can use this book. I can see it transforming lives.

—Dr. Bill Curnow,
L.I.F.E. Coaching International, Wyoming, Michigan

PRAISE FOR
The Missing Commandment: Love Yourself
DVD and Study Guide

The Missing Commandment: Love Yourself is a weighty book, and I am grateful that Jerry and Denise have provided additional materials to help participants in my classes work through each session. Gently breaking up the book into understandable, bite-size pieces is difficult, but Jerry and Denise have done just that. The video provides a picture-story of what happens when portions of your childhood are blended with misguided beliefs. And the accompanying study guide is a well-designed resource for each week, with thought-provoking questions for further inner healing. As a class facilitator, I have found these materials extremely helpful. I feel so blessed that I get to show up and watch God show off through this study and mend the broken pieces in our lives.

—Lisa Franklin,
class facilitator, Arroyo Grande, CA

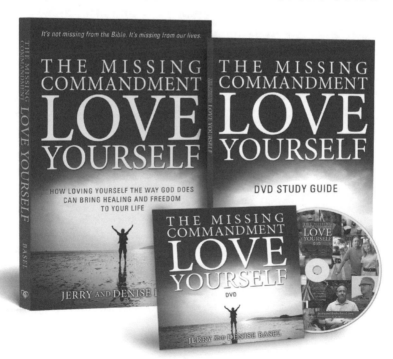

We would love to hear from you. Please email us at jerryanddenisebasel@gmail.com and share your thoughts, reflections or stories inspired by this book or any of our other resources. Thank you.